ADVANCE PRAISE FOR WE TRIED TO TELL Y'ALL

"Digital research and our technological landscape often force scholars to move at light speed toward the newest shiny object, yet Clark's insightful work forces the reader still. *We Tried to Tell Y'all* is the right text—at the right time—with the right author to reflect on the beautiful, complex, and often maddening history of Black Twitter and its relationship to the future of journalism and democracy itself."

—**Catherine Knight Steele**, author of *Digital Black Feminism*

"Based on over a decade of research, *We Tried to Tell Y'all* is the most comprehensive account of Black Twitter to date. Contextualizing it in the broader culture and media landscape, Clark demonstrates why Black Twitter was so significant and so necessary. This is essential reading for anyone who wants to understand the relationship between journalism, social media, and Black resistance."

—**Sarah Florini**, Associate Professor of Film and Media Studies at Arizona State University

"Meredith Clark's groundbreaking new book on Black Twitter masterfully explores the profound impact this digital community has had on shaping discourse, activism, and culture. Through vivid storytelling and meticulous research, Clark reveals how Black Twitter has become a powerful force for social change, amplifying marginalized voices and holding institutions accountable. Her work celebrates the community's humor, creativity, and solidarity but also examines its enduring legacy in the fight for racial justice."

—**Allissa V. Richardson**, Associate Professor of Journalism, Annenberg School for Communication and Journalism, University of Southern California

We Tried to Tell Y'all

We Tried to Tell Y'all

Black Twitter and the Rise of Digital Counternarratives

MEREDITH D. CLARK

OXFORD
UNIVERSITY PRESS

Oxford University Press is a department of the University of Oxford.
It furthers the University's objective of excellence in research, scholarship,
and education by publishing worldwide. Oxford is a registered trade mark of
Oxford University Press in the UK and in certain other countries.

Published in the United States of America by Oxford University Press
198 Madison Avenue, New York, NY 10016, United States of America.

CIP data is on file at the Library of Congress

ISBN 9780190068134 (hbk.)
ISBN 9780190068141

DOI: 10.1093/oso/9780190068141.001.0001

Paperback printed by Integrated Books International, United States of America
Hardback printed by Bridgeport National Bindery, Inc., United States of America

MIX
Paper
FSC FSC® C183721

Dad, I hope I have made you proud. I miss you every day.
Mom, I'm grateful to have your presence and support in all things.
Jonathan, you are my favorite brother.

CONTENTS

As I sit down to write what will be the final words of this book, but perhaps among the first anyone might read, I have a new appreciation for the adage, "charge it to my head and not my heart." Know that if you are or have been a part of my life, and have ever heard me talk about this book or the contents therein, I owe you a debt of thanks.

First, I owe this book to the individuals who agreed to talk with me, to share their experiences, to allow me to consider their tweets and online activity as data. To my collaborators, named and unnamed, I pray you see and hear yourselves in this volume and in my work on Black Twitter. Thank you for honoring me with your stories.

To Robert Mitchell III (@RLM_3), whom I misidentified in my dissertation, I apologize and correct the record here. Thank you for your patience and grace with me.

To every student in my Black Digital Culture, Black Twitter, and Black Popular Culture courses: Thank you for co-creating knowledge with me. Having the space to teach my research while working on it was invaluable.

My dissertation committee, who took a chance on my topic. I am particularly grateful to my advisor, Dr. Rhonda Gibson, for seeing me through the process, and Dr. Daniel Kreiss, for his unwavering support. I am also grateful to Drs. Karla Slocum and Glenn Hinson for teaching insightful courses in ethnography that opened the door to this work.

The Democracy Fund, particularly the Public Square program: Paul Waters, Lea Trusty, Erin Shields, Haneen Abu Al Neel, Josh Stearns, and Tom Glaiser. Your support allowed me to focus on my work, and I am grateful to have been a grantee.

The Park Foundation, for the gift that made my Ph.D. studies possible.

The State of Florida (under Gov. Jeb Bush), for offering a pathway to graduate school.

Sisters of the Academy, for welcoming me out of season and supporting me every step of the way.

The Critical Race + Digital Studies group. It's amazing to see what years of concerted effort can and will do. I look forward to continuing to build with you.

Data + Society, which offered me a connection to the world beyond my apartment during the lockdowns of 2020 and 2021. Special thanks for Sareeta Amrute, Janet Haven, and danah boyd, in particular.

The Berkman Klein Center at Harvard University, particularly the Institute for Rebooting Social Media, for offering space, time, and resources as I worked through a particularly challenging year.

The Center for Communication, Media Innovation, and Social Change at Northeastern University, particularly those who made magic out of a challenging situation.

The Professor Is In, particularly Kel Weinhold, whose writing groups for Black women (and the sisters I met within them) were a haven throughout this process. Thank you for being my friend. I should have said yes to Beyoncé.

The members and staff of the Association of Education in Journalism & Mass Communication.

Natalie Tindall – for offering the advice to "have a backup dissertation topic" when I entered the Ph.D. program – that turned out to be life-changing.

Deen Freelon & Charlton McIlwain - for the collaboration of a lifetime.

André Brock - for doing the work that is essential for Black students' survival in this game.

Siva Vaidhyanathan - for being a tireless and faithful mentor, and a trusted friend.

Yolanda Flores Niemann - for showing me that it's possible to keep it real in academia.

Sue Robinson - for striking all the right notes in mentorship.

Ashon Crawley (and Specklesss) whose friendship is indescribable. As I've said before, I'm no Lorraine Hansberry, but you are absolutely my James Baldwin.

The cadre of digital media scholars whose work inspires me to work harder, including, but certainly not limited to (here's where I *know* I'm about to mess up and leave someone out): Adam Banks, Catherine Knight Steele, Sarah Florini, Al Martin, TreaAndrea Russwurm, Raven Maragh-Lloyd, Ashleigh Greene Wade, Allissa Richardson, Zari A. Taylor, Kiara Childs, Rachel Kuo, Marisa Smith, A.D. Carson, Tamika Carey, Lana Swartz, Kevin Driscoll, Aynne Kokas, David Nemer, Andre Cavalcante, Amber (Hamilton) Alton, So'Phelia Morrow, Lauren Mims, Alyssa Collins, Zakiya Collier, Bergis Jules, Makiba Foster, Tonia Sutherland, Safiya Noble, Rachel Grant, Latoya Lee, Minjie Li, Dani Brown, Sarah J. Jackson, Aria Halliday, Kishonna Gray, Shannon McGregor, Briana Barner, Brooklyne Gipson, Rianna Walcott, Dayna Chatman, Dorothy Bland, Katrina Overby, Gheni Platenburg, Mia Moody-Ramirez, Yukun Yang, Olaitan Ridwanullah, the DocNow and Archiving the Black Web crews, and all y'all I should have called by name here...

My Pelo PhD homies - for helping me stay sane *and* somewhat fit, and offering a place to talk about academic life in a secure space.

My group chats - for keeping folks out of our business.

My sisters and brothers in Christ at the Springhill Road, Southside (Durham, NC), and Rugby Ave. churches of Christ. And my little sister Melissa, and all of my adopted brothers and sisters. Your prayers have indeed availeth much.

My FAMUly, the physical manifestation of the second-best decision I've ever made in life: Shout out to The Crew, the SJCG, the FAMUAN, and the College of Arts & Sciences.

My colleagues from the University of North Texas, the University of Virginia, Northeastern University, and the University of North Carolina at Chapel Hill, as well as the *Capitol Outlook, Austin American-Statesman, Tallahassee Democrat* and the *Raleigh News & Observer*. And the *Bay State Banner* and *AfroLA*.

My sorors of Delta Sigma Theta Sorority, Inc., especially the Tallahassee Alumnae Chapter; 24-2DP, Dr. Janelle R. Baker, Vickee Syes, Allison Mathews, Courtney Leonard, and the Denton (Texas), Charlottesville, Va., Boston, and Chapel Hill-Carrboro Area Alumnae Chapters.

Drs. Valerie D. White, Gale Workman, and Régine Jean-Charles, for modeling the kind of intellectual and academic lives I want to lead.

My lifelong friends, including Karon Johnson, Rebeccah Lutz, Kori Wilson, Cynthia Thomas. And the ones I lost along the way.

My therapists.

Jessie, Jonah, and Julianna - TT's heart in three pieces. I will do anything for you.

My family: the Mitchells and the Clarks, for your love and support. And my in-loves, the Greens, too.

Ashes, Kamikazee, Vixen, Gabe, Spencer, and Foster - my faithful four-legged companions over many years and three degrees.

My husband, the man I risked naming in my dissertation when we were dating (glad that worked out!). But I believed then what I know now: You are God's blessing to my life. Above all, I am grateful that I listened to Prof. Penny Abernathy's advice to marry a supportive partner. You have made all the difference in this life.

I thank every version of myself who brought me to this goal and who will meet me on the other side of it.

And finally, thanks be to Him who is able to do exceedingly and abundantly above all that I could ask or think. To God be the glory for the things (S)He has done.

"If you're not careful, the newspapers will have you hating the people who are being oppressed, and loving the people doing the oppressing."

- Malcolm X

In 2004, my hometown paper, the *Lexington Herald-Leader*, ran a correction for the ages.

It was an apology, printed above the fold on 1A: "It has come to the editor's attention that the *Herald-Leader* neglected to cover the Civil Rights Movement. We regret the omission."

At the time, I was pursuing a graduate degree in journalism at Florida A&M University. I'd taken a circuitous route to the field: As with several previous conversations about my career path of choice, I was dissuaded by several distinct truths about the field: If I wanted to be in broadcast, I would be judged for my appearance; exponentially so as a Black woman. If I wanted to pursue a career in print (this was the era of dial-up modems), I'd never make any *real* money. And then there was the unspoken reality of journalism's relationship with Black America: The American news media could not be trusted to tell our stories. I accepted all of these things as general workplace hazards. One bachelor's degree and two public-sector jobs later, I was back in school for my master's degree in journalism.

As a Black journalist, I joined those who stand in the trust gap between Black communities and the press. Growing up, our minister routinely called the paper "the *Herald* Mis-*Leader*." I have yet to successfully persuade my own mother to keep a subscription. I've sat in meetings and conferences where journalism executives, particularly on the print side, have clung to the notion that newspapers will never *fully* go out of fashion. People will still buy them, they say, because they want a physical record of significant events. I've said it myself. My aging, yellowed copies of the *Tallahassee Democrat* (a former employer) documenting President Barack Obama's first election and inauguration are proof. But I'm also reminded that were it not for the kindness of a family friend who bought multiple copies of the paper that day, we might have missed my dad's obituary.

When Samuel Cornish and John Russwurm, publishers of *Freedom's Journal*, the first newspaper produced by free Black men in America proclaimed: "Too long have others spoken for us. We wish to plead our own cause," their words became the eternal epigraph of Black media in America. Our experience with First Amendment freedom is complicated by news and information denial via slave codes that deprived us of widespread literacy, the legacy of Jim Crow-era educational disadvantages, and a system of media inequalities that have enabled the literary public to construct of Black people and communities as imbecilic, deviant, and slothful. Within the confines of media in the dominant culture, our experience is complicated by the ongoing struggle for representation in the newsroom and culturally competent coverage of the conditions and events that continue to shape our everyday lives. Yet we challenge it with the same communication tools, though different modes of practice, as did our ancestors who wielded the pen, the press, and the airwaves to make sure that the brutal truth and Black joy of our stories was told in our own voices and on our own terms. With the introduction of broadcast-style social media, which empowered "many to many" conversations on the same digital platform, the information flows that were once limited to Black weekly newspapers, niche magazines, beauty salons, barber shops and the Black kids' table in the lunchroom suddenly became private-in-public conversations subject to the white gaze, and for people outside of our communities, Black discourse suddenly became a *thing*. Our banal conversations, jokes, critiques and musings became the subject of interest — particularly to non-Black media professionals with the ability to shape public consciousness about how Black people were using the Internet in ways that didn't conform to the digital divide narratives of prior years. But Black Twitter was Black Twitter long before tech writers published their field notes from shallow dives into Black digital culture. The overlap of new media prosumers and news-workers looking to feed the demand of always on, always available digital platforms simply shaped our mutual understanding of what it meant to be unapologetically Black in social media spaces.

As the youngest member of my paper's editorial board, I joined Twitter in 2008 to live-tweet our endorsement meetings, which, until then, had been closed-door affairs that welcomed candidates and anointed contenders. In the off hours, I watched and listened in on conversations among people on the outer edges of my own social network - other Black journalists, HBCU grads, and later, members of the Divine Nine. I laughed at the jokes, and sometimes hopped on the timeline to explain news media's choices in how we decided what made a story, and how that story would be told. But it was a joke that first helped me realize Black Twitter was a thing; a social phenomenon connected to the news and information of the day, and distilled through the virtues of Black netizens.

Years before hashtags like #SolidarityIsForWhiteWomen or #Black-LivesMatter or #DemThrones caught on, Black Twitter was building its network connections through seemingly banal games and forgettable conversations. Over time, the people who played together developed bonds with others whom they'd never met that would allow the collectives to become the catalyst for social-media fueled social movements, a wellspring of creative capital, and actors within a theory-busting site of audience (inter)activity.

The presence of trust in one another, moreseo that the absence of trust in the media, is what binds hundreds of thousands of Black people around the world to a recognizable phenomenon of discourse and action called "Black Twitter."

There are a few things to unpack here. My journalism background makes me bristle when people refer to **THE MEDIA** instead of the specific medium, outlet or production they're attempting to invoke as part of the blame for whatever social ill they're railing against at the time. While my concept of Black Twitter is grounded in Black folks' relationship to mainstream (i.e., corporate owned, mass distributed) media, it relates to every source of symbolic communication that shapes the public sphere concept of Blackness. Black Twitter's discourse involves a swath of media - from hard news in the print pages of the newspaper to television shows we all watched growing up as 80s babies to webseries you never knew existed.

"Our" is going to take on transitive properties in this book. Sometimes I'm referring to Black people - usually Black Americans who trace their ancestry along the lines of the TransAtlantic slave trade, for the purpose of limiting this scope of inquiry. And as a 30-something, college-educated Black women who is but one major illness or accident away from losing my middle-class social status, my frame of reference is admittedly a bit skewed. But that's how I'm approaching this story. The privilege I enjoy allowed me to first pursue a career in journalism, acting as intermediary between information gathering and storytelling, and now a career in academia, which gives me a little more time to do the same thing with bigger words and more print real estate. To provide a single-sentence qualifier for the analysis that follows from here on out, I interpret Black Twitter from my position as a journalist-turned-academic, and more recently, a Black feminist scholar with the tools and language to take up space in the middle of a Venn diagram where journalism studies, critical cyberculture inquiry, and pop culture overlap.

To understand Black Twitter as more than just the jokes and jabs of Black people on the social-networking site, to value it as an *emergent* phenomenon, we have to understand the conditions that helped create it: the historic, systematic denial of humanity and information that leaves Black people to look to one another for the details necessary to make decisions as we navigate and negotiate our everyday lives. As members on the roll of Black media pioneers like Russwurm and Cornish, Wells and Cooper, John H. Johnson, Earl G. Graves, Sr., and Cathy Hughes knew: We cannot trust mainstream (read: white-owned and operated) media to do it for us.

The origins of 21st century mainstream news media's credibility problem is inextricably linked to the country's denial of Black humanity and inclusion. While technological infrastructure at one time coaxed the public into a codependent relationship with journalism as we once knew it (limiting our options for news and information to the morning and evening papers sourced close enough to reach us with timely information, the radio stations with signals strong enough to accompany us in our homes and on the way to to work and school, and the Big Three television networks we invited into our homes at night), Black networks – sociologically defined – have and continue to operate as centers of resistance, circulating news and information within communities that are overlooked by forces of corporate ownership and the interests of advertisers courting white dollars. From street committees to church bulletins to the Black press, Black people have used whatever tools we have at our disposal to tell our own stories in our own way.

The *Herald-Leader*'s historical refusal to cover the struggle for civil rights is one critical example of the Kerner Commission's prophecy about 1960s-era news media's contribution to the reinforcement of "two Americas, one Black and one White." In the generation that followed the Commission's 1968 report on the civil disorders that rocked inner cities from Newark to Oakland, implicating the news media's failures as contributors to the riots, journalism has openly struggled with its inability to capture a fair, nuanced narrative of what it means to be Black in this country, with specific reference to its failure to attract, retain and promote Black journalists. While a white-owned, white-serving newspaper could economically, technologically and socially afford to ignore the cultural shift of the Civil Rights Movement just one generation ago, the widespread adoption of mobile Internet technology, and the use of online social networks have empowered Black news consumers to collect on the debt owed for systemic failures to cover Black America's rich and complex social existence.

In some cases, this recompense is dramatic; such as the street-level witness provided by hundreds of Black protesters, activists, and everyday social media users who captured #BlackLivesMatter, America's first social-media-fueled social movement for racial justice. But more often — in fact, daily — the online discourses of Black media consumers and producers daily developed our own complex counter-narratives in the form of the online phenomenon known as Black Twitter.

The panic about journalism's death knells - the dot.com boom and bust; the Internet's ability to make "everyone a journalist"; the fall of hard news reporting in favor of infotainment to capture eyeballs and clicks, is of tertiary concern for Black Americans whose representation in newsrooms and social construction in the news have and continue to be deficient, defamatory, and too often, inaccurate.

How do we reconcile our own information needs with systems that were never designed for us? How do we catch up to our First Amendment freedoms when it took 13 more updates the Constitution for the country to formally recognize us as human beings?

These are the questions I wrestle with when I try to explain how Black Twitter is more than an online phenomena of banal conversation, memes, hashtag memorials and protests. Black Twitter is the information product of a generation whose parents and grandparents found their reality absent from the mainstream press. It is the digital manifestation of our ability to use "the master's tools," as our ancestors did, to tell our own stories, presenting them in a spatial, temporal and social site that disrupts mainstream media narratives about Black life in America. Black Twitter is inclusive of the journalists and content creators forced out of legacy newsrooms and onto the web, and the ones who never wanted to work in those environments in the first place. It is constructed of the social relationships that carry relevant information within diverse Black communities. It is the great-grandchild of *Freedom's Journal*; *Ebony* and *Essence*'s grandbaby; the daughter of LiveJournal and BlackPlanet.

Black Twitter is what happens when Black people become the victors who write their own stories.

How Do I Get to Black Twitter?

Like Mercury Retrograde, seasonal solstices warrant only fleeting attention. The summer and winter solstices, in particular, are a reminder of the evolutionary changes to come: longer nights, shorter days; perhaps slightly less chaotic, in the metaphysical sense.

For Black Twitter, however, the winter solstice of 2020 was something truly special.

The Virgin Mary Magdalene @eri_rosay Dec. 5, 2020 ···
Replying to @lottidot @iChanelJ and 3 others

Just wondering... what would be the benefit of the government modifying everyone's genetic code?

▶   💬   30   ↻   109   ♡   3.2K   ↥

pink 💚 @lottidot Dec. 5, 2020   ···

As black people, genetically we are stronger and smarter than everyone else, we are more creative, on December 21, our Real DNA will be unlocked and majority will be able to do things we thought were fiction. Learn who you are as a people 🕯 they wanna make us average

▶   💬   1.8K   ↻   18.1 K   ♡   15.9 K   ↥

After months of lockdowns, a contentious presidential election, and a few celestial phenomena, most of us were looking forward to the passing of the solstice as a more meaningful marker of time, which was lost in the pandemic's monotony. Maybe it was because we were utterly exhausted after a summer which saw a second wave of racial justice protests, or because the sitting administration had filed yet *another* motion to stop counting valid votes, but our collective wariness about the rollout of the COVID-19 vaccine gave rise to another day of Black joy on December 21—the Negro So(u)lstice.

For nearly two weeks, tweets about December 21, #NegroSolstice and #Soulstice conjured a vision of just how expansive Black Twitter's networks had become since the days before non-Black culture writers amplified our online interactions to the masses. Black faces with red laser eyes peered out from below kente-cloth kufi caps to mock the timeline from avatars and memes. Others quipped about Afrocentric provocateurs inverting the Purge movies' central plotline of racial violence. A single tweet in a conversation about vaccine hesitancy had inspired thousands to join into the revelry of imagining a single day when all our #BlackGirlMagic and #BlackBoyJoy would elevate us to our final forms.

Honestly, you just had to be there.

But if you weren't, by virtue of age, or race, ethnicity, language, or of techno-reluctance or fatigue, the good news is, you can at least read about it until you (hopefully) understand. For many, #NegroSolstice in 2020 was a life-affirming signal that Black people were somehow surviving a second year of lockdowns—and with our humor intact. Still, the trend's reflection in some Black media and complete disregard in others (namely, "mainstream" or "legacy" news media) is a summative illustration of Black Twitter. To borrow from media theorist Harold Lasswell, and put in overly simplistic journalistic terms, the 5Ws and an H, Black Twitter is:

WHO: Black people
WHAT: being ourselves
WHEN: -ever we feel like it
WHERE: on Twitter
WHY: because that's what we do,
HOW: with style.

But of course, Black Twitter is so much more than that. From my perspective as a journalist-turned-academic, Black Twitter is, among other things, the cultural creation of a people who have been persistently marginalized by the same influences that shape what we know as journalism in the United States. As a firm believer in the reality that the social construction of news and information in turn socially constructs our world, I see Black Twitter as further evidence of what it means to chronicle the conditions of digital Black aliveness during the Information Age in the confines of the attention economy. While met with silence by general-interest news media, the #NegroSolstice was covered by Black-centric publications including TheRoot.com, a spinoff of a project created by Henry Louis Gates Jr. at the *Washington Post* in January 2008, and Blavity, a digital-first media startup launched by Morgan DeBaun in July 2014. This gap in attention is illustrative of the limits of public understanding of what it means to be Black in America today. What would otherwise seem like a silly story, maybe one that meets the news value of unusualness, was in fact a portal to understanding how Black folks were coping with the realities of the COVID-19 pandemic. A single interaction over two tweets reflected two themes that epitomized accurate news media's influence in matters of life and death: vaccine hesitancy, which is rooted in historical abuses of government power that continue to foster well-founded mistrust among Black people; and misinformation, as evidenced by the first user's response to popular assertions that the federal government was implanting technologies of control through the vaccines. So-called mainstream news media didn't just fail to cover the story; they also missed a critical opportunity to deliver truly breaking news: Black people got our powers on December 21, 2020. Most of us will decline to disclose exactly what they are, but I can tell you that mine helped me finish this book.

A BRIEF DETOUR: ROADMAP OF THE BOOK

This book commits a story of Black Twitter—as a collective intervention on mainstream media narratives about Black life in America in the early twenty-first century—to the emerging body of scholarship on Black digital culture, with an emphasis on how the phenomenon's cultural production relates to news and information. I argue that Black

Twitter is two things: first, a tri-leveled collective of Black people using the social media platform to talk about our lives to and amongst our-selves, with marginal regard of who may be watching; second, Black Twitter is the outcome of centuries of persistent degradation of Black people in journalism and news media. Both of these descriptions are linked by the influence of US news media, the influence of which cannot be understated (Dixon 2017).

Each chapter opens with the story of a tweet that serves as a marker of the central theme discussed within its pages. I historicize each of these themes, aiming to provide sufficient context for people who don't know about Black Twitter or who may have forgotten some of the incidents and episodes highlighted in the book to understand their relevance to the chapter. I then discuss how the limits of US journalism contributed to Black Twitter's discourse of the moment. That said, like all storytellers before me, I am simply an instrument of this research and retelling, and I hope you'll allow me a few moments here and there to discuss how my own orientation to my people and this phenomenon have shaped the work you're now reading.

MAINSTREAM MEDIA AND THE MAKINGS OF BLACK TWITTER

Black Twitter is any number of things. Those who've had mostly pos-itive experiences might call it a community or a family. Others might call it a bullying mob. Most who consider themselves part of it would just say it's fun, entertaining—a way to connect with other Black people, a place to break down the barriers between news/information/gossip and learn about what's going on in the world. From my vantage point as a journalist-turned-professor, Black Twitter is, among other things, a twenty-first-century response to the centuries-old problem of Black misrepresentation in the media that shapes our world. News media pro-claimed 2020 the year of "racial reckoning" as government, commerce, and media institutions themselves began rolling out apologies as they were called out for discriminatory practices. Books about anti-racist approaches soared to the top of the bestseller lists, while workshops and teach-ins created more competition within a cottage industry designed to alleviate white guilt. But a year later, as President Joe Biden made Juneteenth (a commemorative celebration of the day the Emancipation Proclamation was finally read to enslaved Africans in Galveston, Texas), a federal holiday, news outlets began to finally admit what Black people had known all along, and what shows like NPR's *CodeSwitch* dared to say out loud: the response to the 2020 protests was simply "the racial reckoning that wasn't."

To understand why Black Twitter exists, you must understand why Black media exists—from *Freedom's Journal*, the first newspaper published by free Black men in the United States in 1827, to Ida B. Wells's *Red Record*, to the Black press that covered the civil rights movement when "mainstream" papers either wouldn't or hyperfocused on it as a fear-mongering tactic. You must understand why, despite integration and individual-level progress such as the elevation of Black executive editors at news outlets such as ABC, the *New York Times*, and the *Los Angeles Times*, the need and demand for Black-owned, Black-operated, and Black-focused news media—even when these are all different entities—still remains. There is a privileged position among those who've never been deprived of literacy by slave codes, Black codes, or chronic underfunding in public schools—a suspension of disbelief allows them to consider journalism as "the first draft of history." Yet in fact, through a series of factors that Pamela Shoemaker and Stephen Reese (1996) observed as the "hierarchy of influences," most journalism as we know it in the United States is the first draft of historical *fiction*. Most reporting erases and distorts perspectives that do not originate from a domineering culture that insists on assimilation and conformity, and the history of journalism in this country rests on a foundation of racial capitalism that positions Black existence as subhuman. While Shoemaker and Reese's model was developed in the mid-1990s, its application is also useful for interpreting how journalism has systematically erased, distorted, and demonized Black perspectives over hundreds of years. The model consists of five concentric circles—much like the levels of the Earth's substrate, or the layers of a jawbreaker candy—each closing in on the ultimate influence on what (and who) shapes the news:

1. A culture's ideological/sociocultural forces make up the outermost ring;
2. Extramedia forces, such as advertising dollars and other markers of capitalism, historically influenced the size of the "news hole," the extent to which selected topics are covered;
3. Organizational structures, including the makeup of corporations producing news—which possess their own racialized identities and functions—have more intimate influence;
4. Media routines, including source selection, have determined whose voice is worth listening to according to the pattern of their speech;
5. And finally, the journalist themselves has the most immediate influence on developing news reports. Although we are taught reporters and editors are to be unbiased observers of facts, media scholars admit that the training, experience, and perspective to understand not only which facts matter, but how they matter, and to whom, are indeed factors that introduce bias in the news, even when the bias is normalized as "professionalism."

As pointed out by Media 2070, a project demanding reparations in journalism, the exploitation of Black being has been central to journalistic production since the days of the slave trade, when newspapers supported themselves by selling space to advertise the sale of enslaved Africans and bulletins seeking the capture and return of those who dared to escape (Torres et al 2020). Building on this legacy, wares from cleaning products to skin creams capitalized on positioning Blackness as an undesirable quality in the Industrial Age. This imagery advanced a false reality elevated by schemes of Madison Avenue that portrayed a picturesque white world where Black people only made it into the frame to make conditions more comfortable for moneyed whites. The aftereffects of such erasure are evident in the emergence of boutique firms and working groups looking to gain ground with dollars lost among those who don't conform to a white, unaccented English-speaking ideal, yet still have enough buying power to warrant profiteers' attention.

Advertising was essential to the "print hole," supported by the sale of ad space on newsprint's pages. Thus Industrial Age and post–World War II media economies developed to serve the customers with unrestricted wages, access to education, gainful employment, and unrestricted leisure time—that is, white people, first white men and, later, white women. This is the model in which journalists, as so-called impartial observers, were trained. As journalism evolved from vocation to professional occupation, news workers were educated in the same schools that barred Black students for more than ninety years following Emancipation and the short-lived hope of Black Reconstruction. Despite marginal gains in integration, this is the same system that widely continues to train journalists to attempt to suppress anything that is not approved for economic consumption and focus on what matters to an elite, educated class with little consideration of race.

It is this broken system, built on a broken foundation, that requires Black people to create news and media for ourselves, because our stories are rarely fully and accurately told within it. And that, in part, is the work of Black Twitter.

LIMITS OF MAINSTREAM CULTURE'S JOURNALISM

Black Twitter is, as I've mentioned, one link in the history of how Black counternarratives are formed. As Stuart Hall explains in his essay "What Is This *Black* in Black Popular Culture?," this lineage reaches back through links of the knowledge we shared via words in song and storytelling, and further still through the way we have always used our bodies—our expressions, our postures, our hair—to tell stories (Hall 1993). It also pushed us to adopt media tools, including the printing press for Black newspapers, music and talk shows on the radio waves, and Black public television interest shows. Finally, as Catherine Knight Steele has detailed in her work, the legacy of Black counternarratives stretched into expanses of the digital with the Black blogosphere (Steele 2018). Ultimately, the traditions of creating race-first counternarratives have brought us to this moment where we have adopted a social networking platform uniquely positioned by technology and time to talk to and for one another in ways that allow us to permeate temporal and cultural boundaries using memetic memory and digitally enabled retrieval.

I first got the notion to study Black Twitter in 2010 as I was wrapping up my final days in the newsroom of the *Tallahassee Democrat*, the daily newspaper in Florida's capital city. While clicking through the news of the day, I ran across a headline on Slate's homepage: "How Black People Use Twitter: The Latest Research on Race and Microblogging," and was immediately dubious. I entered journalism as a copy editor, part of the last line of defense in the newspaper's quest to produce accurate information. Writing headlines was a part of my job—and one central part of that work was understanding that people rarely read past the headline. Reading through the story, I took issue with two points. First, the author had focused on what one researcher referred to as "Blacktags," or hashtagged phrases that were incongruent with the news of the day, which, by and large, was what Twitter was thought to be primarily used for at the time. Second, in addition to an expert source—a PhD student at Carnegie Mellon—others quoted in the article included Black media elites, such as Baratunde Thurston, a former writer for *The Onion*, an online satire magazine; and Elon James White, arguably one of the forefathers of Black podcasting, and owner of a podcast network. While their insights all rang true, the sum of the article failed to live up to the whole of its parts, and was rightly and resoundingly mocked with a hashtag created by those very Black people using Twitter, and thus, #BlackTwitter proclaimed its own name.

Much like the student in the story that spawned the Black Twitter hashtag, I was also studying the online activity of the hundreds of thousands of Black people on Twitter, albeit in a very different way. I began by looking for us in a completely different place—news media as a chronicler of daily life and shared reality. During the National Association of Black Journalists' (NABJ) 2012 convention and career fair in New Orleans, I began my pilot research with a stack of cards with one straightforward question and two simple commands: "What is Black Twitter? Tell me. Tweet me." I handed out the cards and attempted to interview my colleagues about it. I quickly discovered that even though Black journalists knew about Black Twitter, they couldn't quite explain what it was. As part of my early research, also I conducted a (failed) content analysis searching for stories about the phenomenon, or for stories about Black people on Twitter, period. Finally, having used two methods to address my key research question, I turned to Black Twitter itself, and posted my call for participants online.

WHAT (OR WHO) *IS* BLACK TWITTER?

In order for Black Twitter to exist as an active network, it must first have individual users and contributors. The first is a given; participants must have a Twitter account to be a part of the phenomenon. The second is scaled to the user's own degree of participation. The people I talked to who described Black Twitter had self-selected themselves to varying degrees to be a part of the network. For some, the definition was as simple as being Black and using the web-based technology: "I think all people who are Black and on Twitter as part of Black Twitter," said @f_itlist, a Brooklyn-based blogger. When we first met and discussed her perception of Black Twitter, she was using Twitter to promote her blog about navigating Wall Street as a Black woman. Four years later, she had built solid connections and a faithful audience, and launched a holistic wellness business online. She continued:

> The first thing that comes to mind is like a mafia. All of us are in Black Twitter. Not just the popular ones. We have a crime family mindset. If it's about the women, we all get together. If it's about race, we get together. We're a family. It's just like a stream. It starts flowing, it hits different places, people jump in and they start talking and talking.

@talibhudson, another user from New York, agreed:

> As a people, we can band together. Everybody's opinion in that moment was respected. Then sometimes it's like a dam, like gender issues. It explodes, everyone's kind of knocked down.

Another user, @Sherial, described herself in a way that likely resonates with most Black social media users of a certain experience:

> I do feel like I'm part of Black Twitter. I don't think of myself as an influencer, but I participate in topics that are relevant.

The majority of responses indicated a wide degree of variability in terms of what self-selecting into the larger network actually means. @Karnythia, who described Black Twitter as "a series of neighborhoods," indicated that she fit into more than one of those neighborhoods—what I deem thematic nodes: "I'm probably 'mean girl' Black Twitter. Folks try me, they do, and it's always going to be something."

@MoreAndAgain acknowledged the presences of allies and empathetically minded contributors that are not Black as being part of the larger network:

> I would say that Black Twitter is a community on Twitter that is mostly defined by the Black people who contribute to it. Not everyone who contributes is Black, but they don't define the group. There are Black people on Twitter who don't contribute, they're not Black Twitter. If you contribute, engage with that community, that's Black Twitter. You don't have to be Black, but you also don't define the topics that are talked about, the concerns, the experience of it all. It's defined by the Black people that contribute to it.

WHERE IS BLACK TWITTER?

There is no digital boundary by which one can enter Black Twitter, yet its digital and social infrastructure are quite real. No special knock, no number of honorary invitations to "the cookout" can get you in. For people who've never spent time in true fellowship with Black people *offline*, accessing Black Twitter comes with a word of caution from one of my collaborators (the term I use to describe people who participated in and contributed to this research): "You can find Black Twitter. But you don't want Black Twitter to find *you*."

Black Twitter is visible to keen eyes of the culture and culture vultures. It is not bound by skin color, but by the politics of the skin, as Fanon would say: the language, behaviors, and wisdom one possesses as a result of being subject to the social construction of race, while electing to navigate the intricacies of that existence with a sense of cultural pride. At the height of our numbers, in 2014, Black social media users took to Twitter at a 2:1 ratio with our white counterparts. But each time we're described as being "overrepresented" on Twitter, I'm reminded of D. L. Hughley's 2000 bit in The Original Kings of Comedy on colorblind racists who count the number Black people in a particular space: "If you know how many niggas been over to your house, you racist like a muthafucka."

But difference is central to journalism's epistemological obsession with creating a compelling narrative. And so it was that a handful of writers began to take note of "late-night Black people Twitter," and "How Black People Use Twitter."

CONTEXTUALIZING TWITTER AS A TOOL OF SOCIAL REVOLUTION

Twitter has been credited as an essential tool in presenting multiple perspectives on world events in real time. The micro-blogging platform, launched in 2006, was one of several social networking sites that contributed to a disruptive democratization of mass media in the early twenty-first century. Where mass media corporations and state media outlets once controlled the world's major news sources, limiting what audiences could see and thus believe about the world around them, Twitter allowed millions of people—from activists in the Middle East to disgruntled millennials in the United States—to construct a different narrative about their social realities.

Like the "triple revolution" of the Arab Spring, which was born of existing social networks within local communities, internet access, and the widespread adoption of smartphones (Zhou, Wellman, and Yu 2011), social media–fueled social movements in the United States are less spontaneous than breaking-news narratives often make them out to

be. The series of protests, demonstrations, and globally networked individualism (Rainie and Wellman 2012) that toppled dictators who ruled
for generations in Libya, Tunisia, and Egypt only *partially* resulted from
the electrifying power of our modern communicative ability to speak
to each other, and for ourselves, in real time via corporate platforms
reimagined as a digital public square. To effectively strategize political
and social resistance to institutions of power including media and government, connected communicators in these uprisings relied on both
the (in)visibility and connectivity conferred by social media, and the
collective memory invoked by the use of culturally resonant phrases and
symbols. Democratic (with a lowercase d) activists flipped the strategy
of dog-whistle politics via hashtags, memes, and quips to persuade people to join collective struggles for freedom, equality, and equity among
historically oppressed groups.

Similarly, #OccupyWallStreet and its satellite protests in cities across
the United States brought Generation X's economic anxiety to the forefront. In their study of Twitter as a site for creating networked publics
through the creation and circulation of movement rhetoric, Penney and
Dadas' (2014) cited use of digital technologies, specifically Twitter, as
instrumental for pushing the operation's message to the front page of
news websites. Both movements set a precedent for hashtag activism
that would be revitalized by Black Twitter in the Movement for Black
Lives.

HOW NEWS WAS PRIMED TO REPORT ON BLACK TWITTER

Twitter's real-time, broadcast-style approach to the microblog did
what no other social networking platform had done in the same way:
it offered a "many-to-many" (Shirky, 2008) approach that allowed
everyday people to report and provide commentary in a way similar
to mainstream news media outlets. This commonality links activists
from the Arab Spring to #OccupyWallStreet to the Movement for Black
Lives. Rather than relying on "established," authoritarian, or "authoritative" sources of (dis)information, communicators had a direct line to
anyone else with an account and were only one step removed from those
who weren't connected to Twitter, but followed its affairs via word of

mouth or direct news coverage. Penney and Dadas (2014) detail #Occupy activists' work, building on Jenkins's poignant assertion that "those silenced by corporate media have been among the first to transform their computers into a printing press," a process that has "benefitted third parties, revolutionaries and racists alike" (2006b).

DEVELOPING BLACK NARRATIVES AS A WHITE-BALANCING ACT

Jenkins's alliteration underscores an inherent bias in how both media and academe tend to privilege the perspective of white people when it comes to technology, and, via their own white gaze, center the Other's ability to wield technology as a transformative power in pursuit of Western democratic ideals. Revolutionary use of digital and social media technology to disrupt mainstream media narratives is commonly considered with a whiteness-as-default point of view and thus media scholars, too, can be indicted along with white (read: "mainstream") media outlets and politicians. Feagin (2013) critiques these figures as architects of a white racial frame through which language is used to construct both a hegemonic public and counterpublics.

Existing journalistic standards, including ethical codes, routine practices, and normative views, have long worked in concert to strip humanity away from Black people, whether we are the subject of a story or the person with the byline. *Kansas City Star* columnist Louis Diuguid spoke of editors' blatant attempts to untangle his Blackness from his role as a reporter. During a speech at the Nieman Foundation in 2017, Diuguid recounted:

> I had one city editor, in discussions about a planned series of stories on African Americans moving to the suburbs that my staff of reporters were assigned to do, tell me that I could not edit that important series because I'm Black. To which I quickly retorted, "So does that mean you can't edit any stories about white people because you're white?" He got my point and apologized for making such a racially stupid statement.

The editor's admonition is an example of how white supremacy influences everyday newsroom rituals. But Diuguid's response is, too. In a single comparison, Diuguid showed whiteness as the default existence, validated his humanity and his competence, and contested beliefs about who can be "objective" in their work. This tension is what I refer to as "white-balancing," the problem and practice of trying to center Blackness within the dominant culture. Borrowed from photography theory, white-balancing predates the digital age, and social media. As a multimedia journalist, I learned to take my own photos for articles by first holding up a perfectly white piece of paper to balance or adjust the camera's lens. The camera was designed around white skin as the point of reference. All else—including darker-skinned subjects—is secondary to the white central figure of each photo, even if none exists. White-balancing, as Justin Gomer explains in his book on the topic's relevance to the civil rights movement, is a form of white supremacy that haunts the images we capture of ourselves and the world around us (Gomer 2020). Metaphorically, it marks the persistent discourse about disparity, inequality and the quest for racial justice in America. As a term of juxtaposition, white-balancing describes the nature of being explicitly forced to use whiteness, itself a sociologically contrived creation, to quantify and describe Blackness as an inferior position in social narratives about American life. The challenge of centering Blackness in studies of journalism and media discourse doesn't seem that deep until you realize how often we (Black people) engage in the practice of defending our existence and the fullness of our humanity in a simple phrase: "If _____ had been white . . ."

Black Twitter has created an entire genre of memes that engage in white-balancing, such as retweeting a screengrab of another user's tweet that models a non-Black person enjoying a liberty conferred via white privilege. Sarah J. Jackson, Moya Bailey, and Brooke Foucault Welles detail such an example via their case study on #CrimingWhileWhite (2020). The practices of white-balancing are articulated offline every day, and are just as often reflected in Black Twitter's narrative functions. We use white-balancing to demonstrate the absence of legal, racial, and social justice; to delineate the contours of academic, economic, social, and political disparities; to construct a picture of how the favorable social conditions of white privilege are often lost on those of us without white skin. The term's relevance became apparent to me as I analyzed mainstream and niche media coverage of Black Twitter phenomena. Whether comparing Casey Anthony's acquittal to the conviction of Shanesha Taylor, a young mother jailed for leaving her children in her car as she interviewed for a job, or juxtaposing police treatment and news media coverage of Black shooting victims like Walter Scott with violent white perpetrators like Dylann Roof, Black Twitter's online conversations made plain the seemingly invisible, "objective" differences of our existence.

Through white-balancing, Black actors also create imagery of legal, social, and psychological systems that relegate Blackness as an afterthought. Imani Perry described this in Black Twitter's reaction to the not guilty verdict in Casey Anthony's murder trial:

> I logged onto Twitter precisely as the verdict in Casey Anthony's trial was announced. A good portion of the reactions I read in my timeline were ones of shock and anger. Anthony's lies and her obstruction of police procedure, matched with bizarre behavior after her daughter's disappearance, led to a widespread public opinion that indeed she was guilty of murdering her two-year-old daughter Caylee.
>
> But there was another notable reaction. I read tweet after tweet with the following formulations: Had Casey been a Black woman, she would have been convicted. And while Black women are being jailed for sending their children to good schools, white women who murder children are being let off. (Perry 2011)

As a multimedia journalist, I learned about white-balancing when I went into the field to conduct interviews and, thanks to budget cuts, had to take my own photos to accompany my stories. Before I could take pictures of someone's fifty-year high school reunion or a community group's toy drive, I pulled out a sheet of blank copy paper and held it before my camera. I snapped the shot a few times, adjusting the lenses so that the photo's composition would have the balance intended by the camera's creator. Whiteness, in its technical form, is used as the baseline for determining how shades and shapes are formed via the camera's lens. Thus the tool that offers us visual images, one of the most compelling forms for capturing our reality, is a symbolic yet concrete interpretation of what it is like to be Black in America: routinely subjected to whiteness as the standard by which all else is measured.

THE VIRTUAL REALITY OF BLACK IMAGINED COMMUNITIES

The early stories of Black Twitter, told through the white gaze with a touch of hipster spin, failed to capture the complex performances of Black social identity and coded communication I saw each time I logged in. When first-shift Twitter logged in, our good home-training extended online as people popped in to check on community happenings before heading out to face the day. We rode along as invisible company on one another's commutes. We served as virtual and surrogate coworkers in majority-white workspaces. We aired grievances with graduate school programs and performative diversity measures in academia. We reminded each other of class differences that characterized our day-to-day existences. Our common experiences as Black people elevated the ties of digital literacy, access and online connectivity beyond the "imagined communities" that historian Benedict Anderson traced through the rise of a literate twentieth-century society. And our interactive communiques were more tangible than the imagined audience that teenage Twitter users described to Alice Marwick and danah boyd (2011). Both descriptions fail to adequately capture the magic of what goes on among Black people on Twitter. Linked together by region, school, and profession, (un)belief, fictive kinship, political ideology, fandom, habits, Divine Nine affiliation, and every other imaginable influence that reinforces a sense of common experience among Black people, those of us who were on Twitter in the first years of the Obama administration had imported and constructed our own networks of friends and neighbors with whom we connected each time we logged on the platform.

CHECK THE METHOD(S)

For more than ten years, from my initial interviews in 2012 to my final follow-ups in 2023, I've combined personal observation, in-depth interviews, textual analysis, and Critical Technocultural Discourse Analysis (Brock, 2012) in my studies of Black Twitter. The personal observations were gleaned from my own "incredibly online" existence between 2008 and 2022. As a former columnist, I learned how to work through what I'd seen a week at a time, taking notes about conversations that stood out to me and looking up references to books, songs, movies, commercials, and other cultural texts that helped me make sense of the online interactions that drew my interest. Initially, I sought to understand how mainstream and niche media portrayed Black Twitter. My initial research questions included:

What does the discourse of a linked network of Twitter users tell us about Black representation in this web sphere?

How do Black people in the United States who use Twitter conceptualize their interactions with other Black people in this web sphere?

Which Twitter-based texts are, according to key collaborators, indicative of a sense of community among Black Twitter users?

What are some of the key themes emerging from Twitter-based conversations among Black Americans that have contributed to trending topics?

How do trending topics linked to Black American culture reflect the employment of identity-maintenance strategies among Black American Twitter users?

Most of the participants, whom I refer to as collaborators—because I do collaborative ethnography—were recruited via messages I posted on my own social media accounts, particularly Twitter. Admittedly, this meant that the lion's share of my participants were people like me: Black, cis-heterosexual, college-educated women. Second to this population were Black men of similar backgrounds. Yet many of my collaborators came from diverse socioeconomic backgrounds. Interviewees were poor, working-class, and middle-class. A few were queer. Only two, to my knowledge, were trans. A subsequent project on #BlackLivesMatter curiously brought a number of white people into my research, though their perspectives aren't reflected in this work. As far as geopolitical boundaries go, the scope of my study on Black Twitter is firmly affixed on the United States, but that position also brings the Black Twitter diaspora into view, whether by force—via the so-called Diaspora Wars, aka the hackneyed arguments about superiority/inferiority and a presumed absence of culture between Black Americans and our kin in other parts of the African Diaspora—or by commonality, such as when overseas conversations overlap with what's going on at home.

To provide context about Twitter conversations, I looked to (mostly digital) news media to learn more about how the phenomenon was being covered. In my earliest studies, I analyzed headlines and stories that included the phrase "Black Twitter," as well as stories I selected based on my experiential knowledge of ties to the online phenomenon itself. Even when journalists didn't quite understand what they were seeing, I was able to identify and interpret stories about what Black folks were doing on Twitter based on the language used to discuss the phenomena. Finally, following André Brock's method of Critical Technocultural Discourse Analysis (2018), I considered not only what was being said online, but also the ways in which Twitter's layout and features structured the conversations that were created, shared, heard, and amplified.

All ethnographers lie, as the adage goes, but I must speak this truth: honestly, it was a messy process. I have file folders filled with halfway-finished notes about different incidents; news stories that I saved for later review but can't remember why; interview transcripts that reflect just how rarely people speak in complete sentences. I wrote and revised more than four approaches to this book. For years, I despaired over leaving something out, or missing a critical piece of the story, or getting dragged because I forgot about a significant incident in Black Twitter folklore. One thing I do not apologize for, though, is exercising discernment. There was plenty of mess within Black Twitter that I saw, took notes on, interviewed people about and considered writing up for this research. But everything is not for everybody, and thus, you will find precious little of that mess—including friendship/partnership falling-outs, scams, and various and sundry incidents of fuckery—in these pages.

Instead, what I offer is a definition of Black Twitter: structurally and functionally, it is networks of Black people who engage in the multilayered process of Black Digital Resistance, a process which isn't defined by struggle as much as it is persistence, refusal, and joy. Black Twitter's efforts to report and bear witness to events that impact our community has created a social media phenomenon in which our connections, creations, and information-sharing processes make us into something like a selective filter for mainstream media, with all the appropriate features that a 24/7 digital news source would like to offer to stay relevant with dynamic audiences. Through our interactions we apply our own system of cultural values, underpinned by the generational influence of resistance to white supremacy. Black Twitter serves as a selective filter, offering dynamic counternarrative to mass mediated depictions of Black life in America and throughout the world.

Where cyberspace was initially imagined as a racial utopia, Black social media users are the corporeal attached to the digital culture; (Nakamura 1995) we are the vessels of wisdom and wit by which Black personhood and community is expressed in the online spaces we inhabit. Collectively, we draw on our experiences to speak as something more than a flat, singular "Black community" as described by civil rights leaders of old and the mass media. From avatars to hashtags, to fee-free access and supreme mobility, Twitter's affordances help Black social media users construct dynamic and diverse networks to collectively engage in the ongoing work of racial and social justice via media.

THERE ARE LEVELS TO THIS

Black Twitter's networks of cultural connection scaffold up and across three levels of community—personal, neighborhoods, and the meta-network—each impacted by temporal limits in different ways. Personal communities are the most direct reflection of our offline lives. For instance, a decade ago, when I asked students or audiences why they joined Twitter, they usually told me they signed up because their friends were there. @StarrrDreamer, a participant in the first phase of my research, said she joined at the encouragement of two of her coworkers; the platform created a workaround when they wanted to gossip about other people in the office. The offline relationships are some of the first ones most users recreate online, selectively mirroring offline ties in the digital space. Personal communities are defined by reciprocal follower relationships (I follow you; you follow me), and reflect offline common-alities, including homeplace, that contribute to the shared experiences we have with one another (Gruzd et al 2016). The link between an in-dividual and their personal community on Twitter seems stronger than the "weak ties" most often ascribed to casual friendships and working relationships offline (Brock 2012). Through both online and offline con-versations and ongoing interactions, individuals create affective bonds with other users that of my collaborators, a participant in the first phase of my research, described as "iBFFs" (Internet Best Friends, with an Apple-stylized *i*), and fictive kin:

> I talk to my friends on my Twitter more than people I've known for 15–20 years. And I see other people say that comment a lot: "I talk to y'all [on Twitter] more than my real-life friends." But we *are* real-life friends. Talking to my best friend from middle school is like nails on a chalkboard.
>
> On Twitter, we're in the same fields, have the same professional goals, the same professional life. It's crazy to think about how we have more in common than someone you've known for twenty years. They're motivating, too. *@user* is the big sister I always wanted, never had, glad I never had. She'll *stay* in your ass about something. Ask why I haven't done xyz. She'll post links to motivate me. My friends who have known me forever aren't nearly as encouraging.

As social identities diverge among grade-school friends who've grown up in the same area, due to education, work experience, and per-sonal preferences, Twitter connections help fill in gaps within personal communities. Each level of community connection within Black Twit-ter, no matter how amorphous, is dependent on the user's willingness to participate. In their 1970s and 1980s–era studies of geographically bound communities, psychology researchers including Seymour Sarason and later David McMillan and David Chavis found that there were four key qualities that contributed to a person's "sense of community": (1) an individual's sense of group membership; (2) their perceived influence on the group; (3) their ability to voice their needs and have those needs met, and (4) a shared emotional connection with others in the group (Sarason 1974; McMillan and Chavis 1986). This process is illustrated further in Chapter 4, as Black Twitter was motivated to participate in protests for racial justice, and to serve as advocates and supporters for one another in offline spaces, such as work. Yet as researchers including Anita Blanchard and others have observed, you can't measure the community and strength of social ties between individuals who meet and connect with each other online in the same way that you do for brick-and-mortar populations (Blanchard 2011 Twitter users who log on to participate in live-tweets and other conversations are having their needs met outside the structures of a city block or suburban subdivision.

The People in Your Neighborhood

The second level of community, which I initially called "thematic nodes," is found among those individuals linked by similar interests who regularly engage with one another around specific topics of conversation. Mikki Kendall (@Karnythia) was the first person I spoke to who affixed a more manageable label on these clusters of users: neighborhoods. It's in these neighborhoods that the classic sense of community scale is best applied. Individuals who claim "Black Feminist Twitter" or "Blerd [Black nerd] Twitter" as their home indicate a sense of belonging in these online webs. In freeform and prescheduled conversations and live tweets, these digital neighbors demonstrate a sense of membership and a desire/willingness to belong, as seen in their avid participation in online chats about shared topics of interest.

On Twitter, I primarily move between two neighborhoods, each reflecting a component of my offline life, but with connections that reach far beyond people I interact with at work or in my apartment complex. By day, prior to 2022, I used to fall in with Blackademic Twitter, chopping it up with colleagues whose work, like my own, is governed by the common components of research, teaching, and service. Although I've never been Black Twitter famous, I have occasionally enjoyed the opportunity to contribute to ad-hoc publics: similar structures of online social actors who rally together around a specific cause for a short amount of time, and then go their own ways. However, Black Twitter's neighborhoods endure longer than ad-hoc publics, which is their primary difference. Visiting them is like calling on good friends who live in different parts of the city. But instead of meeting that friend down the block for coffee two or three times a month, we gather together to discuss recurring themes in our lives. My themes, for instance, include Black feminism, natural hair, Black religiosity, news media, and on Thursday nights between 8 and 11 p.m. Eastern, all things Shondaland. It's probably the neighborhood I visited most, tweeting along with the Black girls who also watched "my stories": *Grey's Anatomy*, *Scandal*, and *How to Get Away with Murder*. As Sherri Williams discusses in her book on Black social viewing, tweeting alongside television shows and other media adds another component to online community construction within Black Twitter (Williams 2025).

The neighborhoods also offer intersections between Black Twitter and other online communities, and between Black individuals who consider themselves part of Black Twitter and those who don't. While there's no racial requirement, no paper-bag or one-drop rule about who is denied entry within Black Twitter's network connections, it is fairly easy for individuals who would *not* identify themselves as part of Black Twitter to interact with those who do. Second-screening—using another device, usually a mobile phone, but sometimes a laptop or tablet—to tweet in conversation with users who are simultaneously watching the same program (which sometimes includes the show's cast and crew) is one way social media users who were otherwise ignorant of/disconnected from Black life and culture became more aware of Black Twitter as A Thing.

Gene Demby, from NPR's *CodeSwitch* podcast, which covers cultural history and trends in communities of color, unpacked Black Twitter's role in boosting shows like *Scandal* as a ratings juggernaut in 2013, https://www.npr.org/2013/05/20/185534670/scandal-creates-twitter-frenzy.

It's like watching the Super Bowl on DVR, right? You want to be in the room with everyone kind of yelling at the screen and rolling their eyes and throwing their hands up and saying all kinds of snarky stuff, right? And that's how it is to watch "Scandal," right? . . . You're having conversation with people that you don't know, which always happens on Twitter. But for black people on Twitter, I think there's a chance to kind of worked out a lot of issues or like I kind of have debates in a space that's—these aren't political debates but they're definitely debates about the kind of stuff we all deal with, right? Relationships and whether things are appropriate and, you know, it's just a funny, ridiculous time and it feels like it goes by too quickly.

Black Twitter's neighborhoods, much like our subdivisions and blocks in the offline world, are also sites of disagreement and diverse opinions. Dayna Chatman detailed how fans and "anti-fans" debated the plot points of *Scandal* during its seven-season run, elevating conversation about prime-time representations of Black womanhood as embodied by Olivia Pope (the lead character, played by Kerry Washington) that reflects a range of opinions on what it means when race, gender, and power come clad as a gladiator with a killer body, impeccable education and professional credentials, flawed morals, a flawless weave, plenty of sex, and a penchant for staccato verbal takedowns of anyone who would stand in her way (Chatman 2017). The online commentary inspired by Olivia and Fitz (her married lover, who happened to be president of the United States) elevated viewers to the realm of fans, Chatman wrote, citing Jenkins's definition of an active audience that goes far beyond simple intent and strategic consumption of television. Fans, like the people of Shondaland who weave quips and quotes from the show into everyday conversation, memes, and memorabilia, are the ultimate prosumers— they create alternative narratives and scenarios based on the scripted drama, often immersing themselves into Olivia's world. And where there are two or three hundred thousand of those fans gathered and tweeting together, there is also a distinct sense of community in the midst.

THE META-NETWORK: WHAT MOST PEOPLE ARE TALKING ABOUT WHEN THEY TALK ABOUT BLACK TWITTER

Whether brought together by regular programming, TV specials, hot gossip, or a pithy soundbite from the day's news, users who move between neighborhoods that capture their cultural interests construct only part of Black Twitter's ephemeral community structures. The meta-network, which often captures the interest of news media, offers a large-scale, more nebulous level of connection and is arguably also the most influential in terms of disrupting mass media agendas about Black life in America. It differs from the concept of the neighborhood in three ways: first, by its size (reach), which is constructed via interactivity between smaller personal communities and neighborhoods. Topics of regular conversation among small clusters of users make their way into the timelines of other users who have existing personal relationships with members of a particular neighborhood, and then retweets, hashtags, and general discourse form temporal connections between the two. Second, whereas participants in a particular neighborhood might seek fulfillment via one another's attention and interaction, Black Twitter as a meta-network/set of counterpublics influences a limited public sphere as a whole, as its conversations are amplified through existing mainstream media channels. By tweeting in a way that drives algorithms, and, with them, the attention of media gatekeepers plugged into social media, Black Twitter as a meta-network performs an agenda-disrupting function, forcing professional newsworkers to pay attention to Black prosumers. At best, this attention drives changes in coverage and engagement with Black communities. At worst, it creates an environment in which Black creativity and knowledge production is exploited for profit and notoriety, as we've seen time and again with Black creatives from Peaches Monroe (who coined the neologism "on fleek") to Traptorial creator Wvrthy, whose work creating makeup tutorials on YouTube set to the beat of popular hip-hop music was quickly copied without credit by creators that Black Twitter mobilized to call into account. Third, Black Twitter as a meta-network links users together via their personal communities, and the neighborhoods are typically brought to life by the incendiary themes of the triggering event.

Early in my research on Black Twitter, one user in particular, @FeministaJones, a woman who started out as a private citizen—a social worker and sex-positive blogger who used Twitter to develop a larger platform for activism and creative writing—emerged as a key actor in a critical case that illustrates what Black Twitter's three levels of connectivity look like in action (the case, about mobilizing New Yorkers to participate in protest marches after Eric Garner's death, is detailed in Chapter 4).

Jones is a smoldering, enigmatic presence, both online and off. Standing at least 6′, her frame hooked followers via her #SexyShred workout challenge, but also evoked the catcalls and street harassment that led her to create #YouOKSis, a reminder of how gender-based violence impacts women of color. One of her catchphrases, "purple is a habit," describes her aesthetic. In the years I've known her it's punctuated every part of her look, from rocking braids interwoven with purple yarn, to cat's-eye framed glasses that sport an electric shade of the hue. After years of online harassment, including threats of rape and murder, she limits use of her government name to her offline work and the company of friends and family. Her blog posts, Twitter feed, and online activism—including #NMOS14, a networked vigil for collective grief that preceded the many marches to come in the Movement for Black Lives, and #YouOKSis, an anti street-harassment campaign that centered Black women—has made her the subject of both organized and individualized harassment online. Still, she remains open, honest, and deliberate about her use of the platform.

"I actually signed up for Twitter when my husband moved out of the house," Jones told me in August 2012. "Friends were like, 'you can go on and get your thoughts out in 140 characters.' I'd been on Facebook since it was only open to people who'd been on Ivy League campuses. I was fascinated by the idea of watching favorite celebrities tweet in real time. But I didn't start tweeting for six months." Jones's initial connections on the platform were friends from her offline life—a mimicry of the personal communities she enjoyed in New York City.

"It became a chat atmosphere for us. We'd use anything that cut down on long-distance bills. I started encountering interesting people; started attending events that people posted. I'd go to events, meet people, follow them, it was a cycle," she said, recalling the data plans of yesteryear. Her new chat partners on the platform encouraged her to blog more—posting entries about Black feminism and sex-positivity, topics she returned to again and again in her Twitter "neighborhoods."

Each activity that Jones describes is a point of social and technological connection to her hundreds of thousands of followers on the platform. The chat partners from her old blog and BlackPlanet, as well as her friends from offline life, are part of her personal community, ever since they relied on Twitter to alleviate the cost of long-distance conversations when carriers levied heavy fines and charges each time a user exceeded their data package's limit. At a time when something as simple as working out the details of where to meet friends in the city could turn into a $100 or more cell phone bill, Twitter provided a workaround that helped keep personal communities connected.

Some of the new acquaintances from Twitter-advertised parties and meet-ups became part of that immediate level of connection, too, though interactions with others formed second-level ties connected by the themes resonant in her work—Black feminism and sexuality, social justice, and good old ratchet fun. Being a high-profile Black feminist in the space has also placed Jones in a position of influence within the meta-network of Black Twitter. She's been the subject or center of both of Black Twitter's extremes, from moments of being "dragged" for a litany of perceived slights, comments, or (in)actions, to standing at the center of early mobilization in Black digital activism, which she detailed in her 2019 book *Reclaiming Our Space: How Black Feminists are Changing the World from the Tweets to the Streets.*

Black Twitter's connections are well-explained through the sense of community theory, but the existing framework is limited to an oversimplified, structural explanation for the phenomena. It lacks the descriptive elements that tell the stories of how thousands of Black users with divergent backgrounds came to connect with one another via Twitter and build detailed, delicate webs of friendship; intimate partnership; and conversational salons and spaces for organizing and collective grieving. It places positivist limits on the chemistry and kinship found in the online community and collective bonds that are stronger than weak social ties defining an audience, activist network, or social movement. Talking to Black users who considered themselves part of Black Twitter helped me make out the two highest levels of community connection. And an intimate understanding of the erasure that occurs in mainstream media bolsters my central claim—that Black Twitter, in its most recognizable form as a meta-network of communicators advocating for Black communities in the public sphere, is the embodiment of Black resistance in the digital space. Our conversations on the platform are a private-in-public acknowledgment of our ongoing struggle to have our humanity recognized, our stories told adequately, fairly, and with authentic cultural competence. Twentieth-century theoretical frameworks, including the deficiency-based theories that have described Black technologists as victims of the "digital divide" and infantilized our use of digital technologies in the pursuit of entertainment and pleasure, are ill-equipped to synthesize our use of Black orality, visual elements, and cultural references in the collective service of creating Black counternarratives. Even more modern observations of our technological agency—including descriptions of our online norms and the criticism that without adequate social infrastructure, our social movements are doomed—fail to interpret the Black Twitter phenomenon for what it is. It is a digital connection to our centuries-long history of using the communication channels and tools that we have in the battle against America's original sin of weaponizing literacy and information to mold the Black image as eternally inferior in the dominant culture.

When the Internet Strikes Back

Carrying this burden into everyday conversation and every online ex-
change is too great a responsibility for most of us to consider every
day; we often do it unwittingly, or without seeking a specific outcome.
But centuries of having our collective images warped by every major
source of normative influence in the United States—from Constitutional
amendments to the nightly news—has left us with some stark truths to
negotiate as part of our mediated existence. First, we recognize that every
bit of information is the subject of its creator's influence. As Black people form online communities in the interest of caring for one another,
we yield control of the messages we send to construct our own social
realities—ones in which we are present, equal, and powerful rather than
inferior or erased, as we have been over time. Second, we acknowledge
the lion's share of the information we and our counterparts use to shape
our social realities is, at its inception, shaped by members of the dominant culture. (A concept discussed later in the book explains how we
negotiate this pressure.) Third, as we work outward from our information in-groups, we bring a tacit message for media gatekeepers. That
is, if they want to build and maintain positive, persuasive relationships
with Black communities, journalists and news outlets must examine
the influence their personal experiences bring to the information they
wish to present, and they need to consider the experiences that Black
people draw on as we process that information. These are the principles by which Black Twitter's form—its three levels of community
connection—are constructed. They serve as measures for producing significant, meaningful interpretation of Black Twitter's online discourse,
and its offline influences.

We construct this amorphous, collective, yet contentious online identity via discourse (online conversations), elevated weak ties (relationships with others), and ongoing interaction. Black Twitter exists much
like Black communities in offline spaces: everyone knows we're there,
but except for drawing on our labor or "borrowing" from our culture,
few people bother to engage us directly. Trying to explain Black Twitter to outside (read: non-Black) audiences is like trying to explain the

Black American experience to a victim of colorblind racism (Bonilla Silva, 2011). It's hard for someone sold on the myth of meritocracy to understand how and why the racial differences that we did not construct have become a point of shared identity, and how proudly proclaiming that identity is not an affront to others, but an affirmation of self.

André Brock first described Black Twitter as an exemplar of "cultural conversation" in digital spaces, detailing how the use of Black orality and African American Vernacular English made the adoption of social networking technology more visible in the white gaze (Brock 2012). Sarah Florini compounded this focus on Black Twitter as an ongoing exercise in semiotics, taking great care not to collapse the plurality of identities in her analysis:

> I should be clear that Black Twitter does not exist in any unified or monolithic sense. Just as there is no "Black America" or single "Black culture," there is no "Black Twitter." What *does* exist are millions of Black users on Twitter networking, connecting, and engaging with others who have similar concerns, experiences, tastes, and cultural practices. Black people are not a monolith. (2014)

To an extent, both of these definitions are a good fit for describing Black Twitter, yet I argue that each falls a bit short of capturing the network's specific influence on contemporary mass media, particularly journalism. Like Florini, my standard answer usually focuses on what Black Twitter is not: it is not a *different* place or online space. To build on Melissa Harris-Perry's work (2004) on the barbershops and beauty salons where our conversations originated, Black Twitter exists as a digital cultural commonplace, characterized by our offline experiences navigating the world in Black bodies.

It's probably best for all of us that news media made by and for the domineering culture didn't pick up on the #NegroSo(u)lstice story. After all, there's nothing particularly newsworthy—by the dominant culture's standards—about our shouts of joy from the digital playground. It's also easy to write off Black Twitter as the ineffectual chatter of faceless online mob. But in each case I examine in the pages that follow, we will explore how Black Twitter's online activity quickly transformed from the online phenomena of conversation among several thousands of users "overrepresented" on the platform, to a theoretical process of narrative intervention with direct implications for people's lives and livelihoods. That transformation occurs in six distinct yet iterative phases linking together individual agency and collective identity, turning historically marginalized outgroups into the in-crowd, and demanding mainstream media recognition via collective work and responsibility. Arguably, it is a generalizable process, as witnessed by other groups who replicate the process in their own struggles to use social media as a tool in social and racial justice work. But within the context of Black Twitter its use is intentional, cultural, and practical. I describe it as "Black Digital Resistance."

2

We Wish to Tweet Our Own Cause—Theorizing Black Twitter

The *National Enquirer* is commonly known to most folks as a grocery-store tabloid, infamous for headlines about Batboy, extraterrestrials, and sordid celebrity gossip—the likes of which vanquished John Edwards in 2007 as he set out to challenge Barack Obama's run for the White House. But sometime around 7:30 on the morning of June 19, 2013, a tweet from the paper revealed details of celebrity chef Paula Deen's use of the n-word at work.

Like most of the participants in my research, after years of using the site, I'd developed a habit of checking Twitter first thing in the morning. That day, I scrolled past the tweet, uninterested in the details of another famous white woman's racism, and went about my day. But when I checked Twitter a few hours later, it was clear that Deen was—as my father used to say—in a world of hurt.

S. double-chin V.
@savvyfatty

"Klan Chowder." "Lynchables" "Emmett Tilapia." This #PaulasBestDishes is just...
screaming

↩ Reply 🔁 Retweet ⭐ Favorite ● ● ● More

301   **78**
RETWEETS · FAVORITES

1:57 PM - 19 JUN 13

#PaulasBestDishes, a play on the Food Network TV star's show of the same name, had begun to trend alongside memetic references to

southern and soul-food dishes flavored with a dash of anti-Black big-
otry: "When You Hear White Folks Talking You Better Hushpuppies,"
tweeted @rebel_salute. "Coon on the cob," came from @CerromeRus-
sell. Tracy Clayton, a writer and then cohost of the BuzzFeed podcast
Another Round, retweeted a mention from user @michellej: "Mulatto
Marmalade with High Yellow Biscuits #PaulasBestDishes Too much?"

For Deen, the online spectacle *was* entirely too much. Within days,
she posted three separate apology videos as sponsors pulled their
endorsement deals. Unlike white women in cases profiled by Raven
Maragh-Lloyd (2024) in her work on Black digital practice, who earned
nicknames such as #BBQBecky and #PoolPatrolPaula after being caught
on cell phone video harassing Black people for simply living their Black
lives, Deen's undoing came through the amplification of a networked
game of the Dozens as Black Twitter chimed in with their best jokes. Of
the tweets I collected to code for my earliest research on Black Twitter,
not one mentioned called for Deen to be fired or for advertisers to end
their contracts with her. As @ShareefJackson told me:

> We deal with so much stuff, and there's so much terrible stuff, a lot of
> times we take the humor to laugh to stop from crying—like #Paulas-
> BestDishes or #WhenDoesJustineLand. We use it to keep from going
> crazy.
>   I feel like [for] people in Black Twitter, there's power in saying that
> we are this voice. There's power in saying that we are this community
> of diverse people and experiences, and we have the power to drive
> conversation.

And drive it we did. #PaulasBestDishes kicked off the Summer of Accountability in 2013. In July of that year, @genielauren used the hashtag
when she organized a petition to cancel a book deal procured by a juror
who helped acquit Trayvon Martin's killer, and in August, @MikkiK-
endall's #SolidarityIsForWhiteWomen called out white feminists' complicity in the oppression of Black women with whom they claimed to be
politically aligned. Beyond the humor that Black Twitter found in mock-
ing users like Justine Sacco, infamous for tweeting a crass quip about

not getting AIDS before boarding a sixteen-hour flight to South Africa (#WhenDoesJustineLand), and dishing up humiliation for Paula Deen, its participants had begun to create a networked, online process for demanding offline change. The ability to speak in biting, often humorous, and sometimes coded references allowed Black Twitter to tip the balance of power in our favor, leveraging the most fluid currency in the attention economy: shame. The process is but one example of what I refer to as Black Digital Resistance. Developed out of Black Twitter's tri-level structure and its crossover with time-constrained media-makers looking for their next story, users who positively self-*identify* as Black self-*selected* into conversations about concern to Black communities, often using hashtags to indicate their *participation* in the online discourse as they *affirmed* one another on Twitter and *reaffirmed* the digital conversations in offline spaces. They achieved a semblance of often short-lived *vindication* ranging from public apologies (in cases like Deen's) to short-lived diversity pledges from organizations like the Academy of Motion Picture Arts and Sciences. This chapter details the process of Black Digital Resistance as explained through the narratives of Black Twitter itself. Using cases that span from 2013 to 2020, I argue that while Black Twitter is not the "modern day Black press," it has at times served as a powerful outlet for amplifying Black voices and has created pathways for us to develop and circulate counternarratives about our own Black lives.

WHEN JOURNALISM REFUSES TO MAKE IT PLAIN

It took the Associated Press sixty-six years to tell journalists it's OK to say something is racist.

The *Associated Press* (AP) *Stylebook*, first published in 1953, is colloquially known as "the journalist's Bible." The handbook, compiled by a team of editors within the wire service, is used as a teaching tool in journalism schools and regularly conferred among professional writers, particularly after it began to undergo regular updates to its content and language in the mid-1980s. While some publications may have a complementary in-house style guide of their own, the *AP Stylebook* is considered the authority on language that helps journalists turn information into news—its conventions are sometimes subtle, sometimes quizzical, always concerned with the letter of the law, and shielding journalists and their outlets from libel lawsuits. *AP Stylebook* guidelines are the reason that most publications will not say that Michael Brown or Trayvon Martin were "murdered." The teens' two killers were both acquitted, and the *AP Stylebook* entry on homicide/murder requires a conviction for the latter word to be used. Although studies on the *Stylebook*'s actual influence have produced somewhat conflicting results, its use conforms to what sociologist Eduardo Bonilla-Silva (2011) calls "racial grammar," language that allows journalists to structure news in a way that affords significant cover for "racially motivated," "racially abusive," and "racially insensitive" behaviors rather than risking potential legal action by explicitly calling or labeling someone or something racist.

How Racism Is Embedded in the Cultural Values of News

Journalism's core values, both explicit and latent, are used as a divining rod of sorts, separating reporting and news production that is considered "professional" from a host of alternative forms of gathering and disseminating critical information to relevant audiences. With each iteration of technology and each corresponding shift in the social control of information, journalistic values have evolved from a system of cultural customs passed down from master to apprentice to a set of injunctive norms enshrined as doctrine in journalism education.

As a journalism student in the now-defunct master's degree program at Florida A&M University, I learned the TIPCUP mnemonic as part of a heuristic for defining "news": timeliness, impact, proximity, conflict, unusualness, and prominence were the guiding principles for organizing information sourced via interviews, press releases, written documents, archival sources, and personal observation. A few years later, working with materials created by my colleagues in the School of Media and

Journalism at UNC-Chapel Hill, I taught students to consider a few additional values for deciding what made "news": emotional impact, human interest, and magnitude. I still introduce these concepts during the first week of any news writing course I teach and reinforce them through recitation and writing as the semester progresses.

In my international media classes, I use Herbert Gans's 1970s-era study of US newsrooms to identify the *cultural* news values that American journalists used to decide what would go on the front page of the nation's newspapers, or lead the top of the nightly news (Gans 1979). As the world leader in hegemonic news coverage of international affairs, the M.O. of America's newsrooms continues to impact the way we perceive global events. Gans observed ethnocentrism, small-town pastoralism, responsible capitalism, and moderation as the routine practices American news workers used to influence the information that would help readers and listeners learn more about the world inside our geographically bound communities and in our world at large.

But for decades, Gans has advocated for an approach to news that eschews the process of manufacturing consent for social norms serving the elite in favor of "multiperspectival journalism" that considers how to convey information to individuals of varying social strata, using approaches that make the facts of the day—stock trends, policy decisions, the impact of weather—actually relevant to regular people's (i.e., outside of the economic and political elite) realities. Black Twitter performs this function by filtering information through our own cultural values to interpret *news* as author Carole Rich describes it: information that people use to make decisions in their everyday lives (Rich 2015). This, too, is a form of Black Digital Resistance. Black Twitter recasts news narratives in ways that are historically grounded and culturally accurate.

White supremacy can be observed in mainstream media in journalism's ability to overlook, discount, and/or mischaracterize how Black people have been systematically disenfranchised from participating in the social construction of American reality, from deprivation of literacy (via enslavement, Black codes, and segregation) to persecution and misrepresentation by and in the press. In the digital age, one of the ways such racism is perpetuated is through news stories that frame our Black use of technology from a deficit—such as the early observances of Black Twitter that described our online activity as an oddity. Another is through the absence of contextualizing information. A third is the exclusion of Black voices. And a fourth is the overreliance on sensational headlines and misleading use of images to lure in readers and viewers. This history, and these contemporary practices, underscore Black Twitter's significance as a journalism and media phenomenon.

THEORIZING BLACK DIGITAL RESISTANCE

The conversations and interactions that occur within Black Twitter actively produce counternarratives that challenge the dominant media frames about what it means to be Black in America in the age of social media. This process, which I refer to as Black Digital Resistance (BDR), is, at its essence the practice of unapologetically living out our existence as Black people, sometimes in the intentional defiance of the white gaze, using social media technology to create, communicate, and build with one another as we exist in disparate physical, social, and economic spaces.

In its best moments, Black Twitter engages with a collective, community-centered ethos, developing a range of discourse from intimate conversations to banal debates, to social viewing and memetic play that create counternarratives that center Black perspectives to challenge mainstream media's depiction of Blackness in the contemporary age. These interactions are first and foremost a quotidian narration of Black life and experience in twenty-first-century America; they're the conversations that anyone, anywhere might have on any given day. But in a media ecosystem where race and class have created information boundaries between Black communities and the mainstream media—conducting these conversations in the larger public sphere is in itself a political act, which is what leads me to refer to it as a process of Black Digital Resistance.

Until social media—particularly Twitter, with its broadcast-style model—placed the world in open conversation and open-ended publication mode, Black-centered media narratives were rendered invisible by others outside of our communities. Weekly newspapers, monthly magazines, urban radio shows, and TV sitcoms centered around the lives of Black people are all accessible to anyone with the motivation to look for them. But Twitter's cacophonous, many-to-many conversations placed Black discourse alongside the mainstream, and, suddenly, our conversations became increasingly influential and forced media gatekeepers and others to check their perceptions of Black images.

The process of Black digital resistance is, quite simply, the act of being Black in a mediated space, and recognizing our individual and collective power through communication. It requires self-selection by users who identify as Black and/or are connected to issues of concern among Black communities. It moves everyday conversation from individuals and personal communities to collective action among thematic nodes that are affirmed through retweets, quote-tweeting, and favoriting online, and reaffirmed offline through the sharing of culturally resonant ideas and phrases through memes. Black Twitter's power is then vindicated through increased and more culturally competent media coverage, replication within other demographic groups, and spin-off hashtags that serve as mediators of Black culture in the virtual and real worlds.

Self-Selection

By elevating Blackness, which has historically been categorized as an out-group, and purposefully addressing personal experiences within that out-group as a way to build and maintain a positive, cohesive, and diverse identity, the social media users who make up Black Twitter collectively position ourselves as an in-group with common history, struggles, and triumphs. Our individual concerns may be different, but we foster cohesion through a sense of collective responsibility for the health of Black communities. In this chapter, I chose to focus on a singular, social-activism oriented aspect of Black Twitter, which presents itself as an expression of collective social identity maintenance work, rather than exploring more lighthearted takes.

By joining in online conversations across thematic nodes via Twitter as self-selecting, positively self-identifying Black persons, participants are claiming an identity for themselves individually and collectively. Our identity-maintenance work includes a sense of community responsibility to include and protect smaller, positionally weaker groups who otherwise might not have the same level of representation. Unless the topic of conversation divides Black participants into specific ideological or demographic groups (i.e., how #BlackPowerIsForBlackMen highlighted a rift between Black men and Black women, and furthermore Black feminists and Black women who do not identify as feminists), this sense of positive Black racial identity is cohesive enough to include individuals who might otherwise be split along fault lines including education, socioeconomic status, and political ideology. The external events that triggered Black Twitter to mobilize generally positioned Black people as an out-group. #PaulasBestDishes and, a few days later, #PaulaDeenTVShows, used soul food and entertainment metaphors to satirize stereotypes of Black people as subservient. Several of the people I spoke with mentioned the helplessness and injustice they felt in the aftermath of the verdict in the George Zimmerman trial, which motivated them to participate in conversations about Juror B37's CNN interview and pending book deal, use "JurorB37" (with or without the hashtag), and sign the related position to get the juror's contract canceled. The Juror B37 saga was an early act of digital accountability practice, a theme I explore more in Chapter 5. The two key collaborators with direct ties to #SolidarityIsForWhiteWomen spoke of how, as Black feminists who advocated for Black women, their presence and experiences were trivialized, ignored, and blamed for "derailing the conversation" on feminism. These external events influenced participants' decisions to bring their perspective and social realities to the conversations happening beyond their personal communities. By using their Twitter timelines as an echo chamber of sorts, Black Twitter participants indicated their willingness to self-select as a process of participating in the phenomenon. The decision to self-select into these race-centric conversations is inextricably linked to the users' identity as part of an existing out-group. Before moving on, I must reiterate that the process of Black Digital Resistance does not necessarily proceed linearly, though this is how I explain it. For instance, it's possible for someone to see a hashtag in an offline space and work their way backwards into the online conversation.

IDENTIFICATION: RECASTING BLACK SOCIAL IDENTITY

According to social psychologists Henri Tajfel's thesis of social identity and group behavior (Tajfel et al 1974), people who are social outcasts in the dominant culture (the out-group) use certain strategies to elevate and reposition themselves as part of a desirable group (the in-group) (Tajfel et al 1979). Dannagal G. Young explains this theory in terms of sports teams and their fans' us-versus-them attitudes in her book *Wrong: How Media, Politics, and Identity Drive our Appetite for Misinformation* (Young 2023). When individuals who are marked as part of an out-group work to develop their own positive, affirming group identity, they must recognize both the perceived threat against their group and the belief that through group involvement, their out-group can change its position.

To put this theory into a more Afrocentric context, I began to examine the process of social identity development/maintenance—in other words, seeing oneself as part of a community, and thus part of the solution for elevating that community—through the work of Mauluna Karenga, who created the seven principles of Kwanzaa (Karenga 1995). Two principles in particular—kujichagulia, the principle of self-determination, and ujima, collective work and responsibility—are useful and more culturally appropriate for understanding practices of Black community formation (Harvell 2019). The former means "to define ourselves, name ourselves, create for ourselves and speak for ourselves." The latter is to "build and maintain our community together, to make our brothers' and sisters' problems our problems too, and to solve them together." These concepts are particularly useful for understanding the power of communication among Black social media users enacting a sense of shared identity when digital spaces such as Twitter are thought to sever the connection between racial identity, cultural practice, and the body.

Nearly in tandem with identifying as part of the community, one becomes part of Black Twitter when they become active contributors to the community's welfare. This happens when they contribute to conversation about issues of interest to and from the perspective of Black people, and spread those messages via retweets, hashtags, and mentions. In the midst of the "summer of accountability," @Blackamazon spoke about how participation in the conversations that tend to activate the Black Twitter network requires a sense of identifying with the community and taking on responsibility for its representation in the media.

> What contributes to that critical mass is that as African-Americans we often see ourselves underrepresented. When stories are reported, there might be something missing that's important to our community. When something comes out that's offensive or ignorant, Twitter is one of the places where people can pick up on that and speak back about it. If something happens and I talk about it at a function or a barbershop, the conversation doesn't go beyond that room. It's about bringing things to the forefront that otherwise wouldn't be. I don't think that we do it for mainstream news. It's to bring it to a wide audience. Not "I hope CNN brings this up," It's a nice side benefit to these conversations. Part of being in a community is loving and defending them, because no one else does it.

Her response is indicative of how Black users recognize our power via Twitter-based conversation. In self-selecting into Black Twitter, participants react to mediated depictions of Black people and our shared realities, as well as our perceptions of ourselves. For Twitter users like @moreandagain, who created the petition to stop Juror B37's book deal, self-selection manifests as "loving and defending" Black folks, rallying the resources available to her to intervene in a process that the family may not have even known about, nor the energy to fight. For users who joined into the #PaulasBestDishes and #PaulaDeenTVshows hashtags, self-selection meant opting into a trend about workplace racism and outright aggressions in a way that allowed the user some levity, as it did for those who chimed into the conversation of #SolidarityIsForWhite-Women, about the exclusion they faced within feminist communities. Black Twitter developed deft techniques for responding to disrespect and depravity, as individuals joined in call-outs of harmful behavior that would eventually be derisively labeled as "cancel culture" a few years later (which I discuss in Chapter 6).

But the critiques aren't limited to a Black-white binary, nor do they all focus on individuals and contexts outside of Black communities. Internal characterizations lead to the creation of light-hearted hashtags like #BlackParentQuotes, where Black Twitter recalled common catch-phrases from our childhood. While seemingly benign, the conversations indexed by these latter types of hashtags can also be interpreted as a defensive strategy, wherein Black Twitter speaks about our private experiences in public, presenting a direct, intimate narrative to counter existing perceptions of Black culture.

PARTICIPATION

The identification stage culminates as one moves from simple conversation in personal communities to a certain degree of self-actualization as a part of Black Twitter. Participants initially tweet to add their perspective to a discussion. But through ongoing interactions, they increasingly grow aware of the commonality of their experience among other users. They identify as part of the structure, and recognize their ability to have influence within that structure (McMillan and Chavis 1986). I found this process of becoming Black Twitter clear in the immediate responses to the question "who do you tweet for?":

"I see myself tweeting for ME" (@PresidentialHB)
"I tweet for myself" (@FeministaJones)
"I'm tweeting for myself" (@IAmTiffJones)
"I tweet for myself" (@F_uitlist)
"I tweet for myself most of the time" (@rdjenkins83)
"I see myself tweeting for me" (@MoreAndAgain)
"I tweet to entertain myself" (@Wribrarian)

Yet each person I asked this question concluded their response in a way that indicated they weren't only tweeting for themselves. Their complete answers, taken verbatim from their respective interview transcripts:

I see myself tweeting for ME. I like to talk, and I like to think that everything I say is important. Since I know someone is following me, I'd like to think that someone else might think it is important. It depends on what I'm tweeting about. There are times that I post something that I want certain people to see. (@PresidentialHB)

I tweet for myself. There are times that people tell me I'm tweeting for them; they couldn't articulate themselves or put themselves out there. I may represent people, but it's not an accurate representation to say I tweet FOR them. I tweet my thoughts, my experience. By retweeting them, it's the ability to say something through someone else's words. I look at retweets and say "that's what I would have said." Sometimes I tweet for those people. Which is pretty awesome. I represent a faction of Black women who feel like they've been ignored. Because of the following I have and the conversations I have, I'm able to talk about them. (@FeministaJones)

I'm tweeting for myself. I'm only tweeting for me. I see tweets all the time that say, "I tweet for (this crazy group of people)." But I'm not here for that. If you do that, you open yourself up to represent that group. I'm not representing diabetics, natural hair and the 30-plus crowd. (@IAmTiffJones)

I tweet for myself. I tweet for Black women who don't necessarily fit the Black Twitter circle. I don't follow the Black Twitter circle for a reason. (@f_uitlist)

I tweet for myself most of the time—from anger, or to space off for part of the day. I do not take myself seriously. Most of the people who respond can relate to what I'm doing. (@rdjenkins83)

I see myself tweeting for me, for anyone who feels like they are engaging with others. (@MoreAndAgain)

When I first started, I found that I was tweeting for and to people in my newfound profession. I was trying to talk to them and network with them. These days, I tweet more for entertainment purposes. To entertain myself. (@Wribrarian)

These responses indicate that my collaborators have an imagined audience, a discrete and textually situated group with whom they interact online—even if only in their own minds (boyd and Marwick 2011). Several clues in their responses indicate that linguistic and stylistic cues from others contribute to a more concrete conceptualization of who is in that audience (Scheidt 2006). The pre-existing ties that helped them create personal communities upon and soon after joining Twitter ground these users' concepts of just who their imagined audience is—people like them. On the whole, the people I spoke with indicated that part of their imagined audience is a larger network of Black people with whom they feel a connection and an ability to influence. When respondents @FeministaJones and @F_uitlist spoke about Black people on Twitter and their representation through one another's tweets, their observations echoed statements that others made about how tweets and retweets relevant to Black experiences contribute to the formation of online communities.

Interpreted via the Afrocentric value concepts of kujichagulia and ujima, these connections provide a tangible, textual forum for the public process of affirming Black people and Black interests as significant. As one of my collaborators said, "Black people have been hurting. Been hurting for some years. If they are given a valve, a way to express that hurt, they're going to take it" (@Blackamazon).

Another user agreed: "I think of Black Twitter as a space where Black people can express and be ourselves among other Black people," @duskyjewel told me. I would call it a powerful, parallel Twitter. It's a place for Black people to read and speak to each other. If it's Black people talking about a particular subject, it's Black Twitter."

As the larger connections form—moving beyond the thematic nodes and into the space where data points from individual timelines converge to create national trending data indicating that there is widespread conversation—users begin to take notice of the power of Black Twitter as a network, and identify themselves as part of that collective.

"Black Twitter is more active and more defined when there is a larger issue at hand. So when people are talking about R. Kelly or Nelson Mandela, things that are relevant to Black people, that's when I tend to see

more about Black Twitter," @duskyjewel said in our interview. As users
begin to solidify their roles as part of Black Twitter, they recognize the
structure as a space for conversation where depictions of Blackness can
be competently analyzed from authentic perspectives. @rdjenkins83's
comments solidified my interpretation of this step of the phenomenon
when he discussed the relevance of the Black lived experience to Black
Twitter's discourse.

> How can you insert yourself in a conversation that you don't live from
> day to day? . . . It's kind of different when Black people talk about Black
> Twitter versus when other people are talking about it. (@rdjenkins83)

Identifying with the experiences of other Black users is key in acti-
vating the network itself. In doing so, users speak for themselves, and
defend their online community as an in-group rather than the out-group
it is perceived to be in the physical world. As they make this identification, they begin to compose deliberate, targeted tweets, including
hashtags that can help quantify the scope of Black Twitter's network
connections.

However, in some cases, Black Twitter's participation, the issuance
and retweets of tweets, occurs around specific subjects of interest
that have been framed negatively in the news media. The folks I
interviewed see these performances as examples of Black Twitter's
activity.

People don't say "Black Twitter brought that to the forefront"; they say
"people are being mean to you on Twitter. What's going on?" The mainstream media finds a way to separate the controversy from the people
who create it.

> When I heard about the woman who tried to get the book deal shut
> down (@MoreAndAgain), they tried to make it sound like it was one
> person who was disgruntled instead of a network. That's the beauty
> of it. There's not one leader. There's a project manager for each cause.
> We were all hurt, and she led the charge. The mainstream story was
> not the legitimate story. I know people who know her. Things aren't
> properly credited to Black Twitter as an entity (@RLM_3).

Cultural studies scholars might describe this part of the process as "performance." My own experience is that when a Black person does or says something in a public space and that action is covered in news or other media without context for a culturally competent interpretation of their "performance," that act becomes something that is inherently bad. @ShareefJackson, however, expressed a positive countersentiment: "I'm of the mindset that if I'm Black and I'm doing something, I'm doing something Black." For Jackson and other people within Black Twitter, participation in the culturally nuanced conversations is a means of expressing a cohesive social identity, one that affirms Blackness from the physical to the digital and vice versa.

Affirmation

Without the physical and cultural communities that establish some of the preliminary ties—such as neighborhood landmarks and street names, high schools and colleges, houses of worship, and membership organizations—it might be more difficult for individuals to define their personal communities online. The same is true, to an extent, of the neighborhoods in which Black Twitter participants form key connections. Many individuals connecting around/within Black Twitter's neighborhoods have offline communities or other electronically mediated spaces (i.e., they comment on podcasts and blogs or connect through more personal communications, such as text messages, group chats, and email) in which they reinforce their online ties in the physical world.

Offline spaces serve a secondary function in the formation of Black Twitter. They are the spaces that participants return to in order to affirm points of conversations that have taken place in the Twittersphere. Here, language, symbols, and cultural practices common to Black physical-world communities are used to validate the ongoing interactions of Twitter users, nonusers, and texts relevant to Black Twitter's conversations. Here, individuals can present their arguments and personal experience from the Twittersphere and subject them to analysis with like-minded members of their offline personal communities for confirmation. Affirmation, in this stage, is a matter of having one's personal voice heard—whether the Twitter user has participated in larger online conversations about a topic or not. By surveilling and sharing, participants in Black Twitter's active meta-network can take bits of the online news and cultural conversation into their physical spaces and confirm its validity and relevance in a way that is liberated from the frenetic pace of Twitter-based dialogue.

Hashtags are indicators of cultural competency in affirming the messages circulated within Black Twitter. My collaborators alluded to this practice when they told me about the offline conversations they've had based on Twitter exchanges with members of their personal communities, partners in their thematic nodes, and other participants across the Black Twitter network. #FastTailedGirls/#FastTailGirls is one example: in 2014, @karynthia (Mikki Kendall) and @thewayoftheid (Jamie Nesbitt Golden), two Chicago-based writers who cofounded the site Hood Feminism, were having conversations about the construction and exploitation of young Black girls' sexuality, and came up with a plan to hold an online discussion.

> If I did a chat for #FastTailedGirls as part of a greater discussion of Black women's sexuality, would y'all participate? (@Karnythia, November 29, 2013)

The tweet was retweeted more than a dozen times before the conversation took off at its scheduled time the next day. The #fasttailedgirls (and the off-keystroke conversation I wound up following, #fasttailgirls) tweets continued to pop up long after the initial discussion, conveying reflections of personal experiences from Black women who shared their experiences:

> #FastTailGirls oh man, all the pregnant teens called up to the front for "prayer." NONE of the dads, and they were there! (@godivabap, November 30, 2013)
>
> I never associated #fasttailgirls with rape. (@aliention, November 30, 2013)

> Little Black girls are under assault, but do we believe them when they reveal their traumas? Bit.ly/1ak8Z0x #FastTailGirls. (@Evette-Dionne, November 30, 2013)
>
> #FastTailGirls Walking to a friend's house and someone mistaking you for a prostitute, no matter what you're wearing and how old u r. (@HoodFeminism, November 30, 2013)

As @thewayoftheid told me:

> It's time to talk about what happens when you're an adolescent girl. It's a matter of getting out of the idea that women or girls bring this on themselves. Everyone has a #FastTailedGirls story. It's ingrained in us. It started that night: we had a conversation on Twitter, I wrote a piece for XOJane. A little while afterwards, we had the scheduled chat. Growing up, you don't realize how much we go through. There were detractors, people who said we were demonizing Black men. [But] It was cathartic for people to know that they were not alone. You're dealing with men who are predators.

The hashtag refers to a colloquialism that polices Black girls' bodies and behaviors—long before they reach an age of physical, intellectual, and sexual maturity. Where the politics of Black respectability required the type of temperance that neutralizes a range of sensual and sexual gestures or behaviors, Black mothers, grandmothers, and aunties sought to protect their family names and girls who wore them by labeling any remotely coquettish behavior as "fast"—an all-encompassing euphemism that signaled everything from the physical evidence of puberty to any sense of sexual agency. If "fast" is a way of being, then having a fast tail is its embodiment, bound up in the flesh of our backsides.

The term absolves others—usually men and boys, but implicitly, the other people who use it as a pejorative—of a responsibility to respect Black women's bodies as our own sites of representation rather than sites of their subjective pleasure. It performs double duty by simultaneously shaming Black women and girls along two planes: the physical—our possession of well-rounded and pronounced curves, dressing in ways deemed inappropriate, acting and speaking in ways that reflect even a hint of worldly knowledge; and the cultural—the invisible weight of having to constantly check that we aren't carrying our physical attributes with an undue modicum of pride. To be fast-tailed is a combination of knowing what you have and using it in a way that suits you—an unacceptable choice for Black femmes who are constantly monitored, scrutinized, and critiqued as representations of our communities rather than simply agents of self. Girls who physically mature early are marked "fast." Teenage mothers are "fast." In order to meaningfully participate in the conversation of #FastTailedGirls/#FastTailGirls, Black Twitter had to recognize and understand what the reference meant based on their own experience. In a sense, these and other hashtags served as a shibboleth, one built on culturally resonant words and phrases.

But as useful as it may have been to hold the conversation online, @thewayoftheid also noted the blowback that came from using Twitter, particularly via journalists seizing upon the conversation and amplifying it by covering the conversation without proper context:

> [We held it on Twitter] I guess because we use Twitter more than FB. We both had a wider reach. I tend to avoid Facebook because my friends and relatives are kinda crazy. It might be better to have this conversation with people you don't know. We wanted this conversation to happen in the open.
>
> That did happen, I wasn't too thrilled because when they did that, of course they left the gates open for R. Kelly supporters to come through and take a dump in my mentions. It definitely happened to Mikki too. She was the one who sort of re-broke the story back then. She used the tweets without contacting Mikki. Put her in a precarious position. You're getting flooded . . . She asked the writer to take down the tweets. After a little pushing and cajoling, the damage had been done. You're already having this very heavy conversation, and now you're having to deal with this other fire that you didn't ask for. We got a lot of unwanted attention.

Having the #FastTailGirls conversation via the relative privacy of a coded cultural reference, but on a widely accessible platform like Twitter, illustrated the importance of disrupting the mediated cultural forces complicit in exploiting Black women's bodies and minds. It is Black women's willingness, and our technologically enhanced capabilities, to expose the wrongdoing that harmed us before we became women, and to trace the systems that contributed to that harm, now that we have the words and tools and ways of seeing. It is the ability to engage in disruptive discourse in ways and places that force others outside of our communities to take notice, and in some cases, action. Our stories, once contained to our physical neighborhoods, radiated outward through word of mouth via #FastTailGirls, boosted by Twitter's affordances to exponentially expose a potential audience of thousands. This form of affirmation meant that our voices were finally being heard as we made visible the hardships and oppressions we face at the intersections of race, gender, class, ability, and access. In conversations like #FastTailGirls, we found a useful tool in the net's abilities to bring our physical networks closer together. Whether we were deemed fast ourselves for growing breasts at an early age, or survivors of the social vulnerabilities of Black women and girls who lacked sufficient standing in mainstream media narratives to be constructed as worthy victims, Twitter gave us a common gathering place to deliberate these issues with greater attentiveness to their complexity. #FastTailGirls and hashtags like it, created in discussions that originated online and used between the virtual and the real, serve as markers of cultural competency for individuals moving between both worlds as we interpret and extend Black Twitter's private-in-public conversations.

Roles of Private-in-Public Conversation

Media sociologist Michael Schudson (1997) says that private-in-public conversations consist of dialogue undertaken to the end of addressing a common problem in a way that is agreeable to the involved parties. The private-in-public conversations that initially take place among Black Twitter's participants online are generally characterized as problem-solving discussions. The #FastTailGirls/#FastTailedGirls conversation, for instance, focused on confronting Black social norms that contribute to the hypersexualization of Black girls and women.

The hashtag-driven extension of Black Twitter's private-in-public conversations into physical-world spaces also fits Schudson's definition of sociable conversation, in which the participants expect that sharing information will reinforce their preformed views. Sociable conversation centered around Twitter-based discourse that takes place within the physical world gives the user's online/offline conversation partners an opportunity to test their opinions with the assurance they are being shared within a space where fundamental values are still agreed upon, allowing participants greater freedom to disagree.

Reaffirmation

To describe the next step, reaffirmation, I return to one of the hashtags that defined 2013 as the Summer of Accountability: #SolidarityIsForWhiteWomen. This hashtag was also created by @Karnythia (which she writes about in her book *Hood Feminism*). During an interview in December 2013, I asked her to tell me about what happened the day she created the hashtag, and how it was received going forward.

> I was defending Sydette, [@BlackAmazon]. Hugo Schwyzer admitted that he'd been deliberately targeting a friend [Sydette]. _____ made an offhand comment that she didn't call him out. And I got mad. Things happen when I get angry. In this case, I'm one of those people who will hashtag things because I'm a person who thinks of catchphrases. It ties in with things that I do verbally.
>
> I thought I was going to have a conversation with people who were experiencing the same things. ____ was not the one who started it. I've written well before this, about racist feminism and that sort of thing. We were probably about a half hour or so into it when I realized we were maybe speaking to folks who were not our group [i.e., Twitter users in her personal communities or neighborhoods], and that people who were not part of the group were still there for the conversations.
>
> I will probably be answering about #SolidarityIsForWhiteWomen until my dying day. I had a couple thousand followers. I expected it

to spread a little bit. I was not expecting to find people who I have no idea who they are, they have no idea who I am, how the hashtag started. It was interesting to see how many people from how many places it reached.

It was strange, the hashtag grew and grew and grew, and there were articles, and it was amazing that there were so many people who were willing to say "hey, hold on, that came from that person."

Once the hashtag got attached to programming and talks about problems that were discussed and going backward. [Like saying we were] mean to white women—it was going backwards. If we're talking about racism, we kind of have to talk about race. I don't want the rest of my life to be about this hashtag. I was doing things before it, I'm doing things after it.

Through reaffirmation, the hashtag lived on for years following its creation. For example, when the Dream Defenders—a group of Florida youth activists of color who occupied the governor's office as part of their protests for Justice for Trayvon Martin (#J4TM)—held their first conference, one of the sessions was titled "#SolidarityIsForWhiteWomen." The session, a panel discussion featuring young women who were prominent in the group's social activism activities, extended the initial online discussion, applying it in a related context as an offline, secondary affirmation of the need for intersectional discussion around gender dynamics, racism, and power. Additional tweets and retweets from those discussions, as well as tweets and retweets from individuals familiar with the initial Black Twitter-mobilized discussion, created a secondary layer of confirmation of the hashtag's significance and cultural resonance, an articulation of the reaffirmation stage of Black Digital Resistance.

That same discussion could have been held with a different title—certainly with one that did not use the hashtag. But inclusion of #SolidarityIsForWhiteWomen in the conference is a reflection of the power in transferring meaning from the virtual to the real and back via the use of hashtags as cultural artifacts. By using hashtags and hashtagged conversations offline, Black Twitter participants create greater permanence for the extension of cultural conversations. It is a practice similar to sharing a message heard first in a different public forum, such as a graduation speech or classroom lesson. Audiences are expected to be receptive to the message because it was initially communicated in an authoritative space.

We can assume that the Black Twitter participants/Dream Defender members responsible for building the discussion around the hashtag in the physical space of the panel discussion did so knowing that the fundamental value in the opinions and roles of women of color would be upheld in the panel discussion, even if there were individual-level disagreements. This made the offline panel discussion a safe(r) space for affirming the views initially expressed via online conversation, giving the hashtag greater permanence among this group of offline participants. The discussion also helped cement the hashtag as a cultural artifact recognizable in the minds of both Black Twitter participants and individuals with no knowledge of the initial discussion. As the panel participants tweeted about the proceedings using the hashtag, they reaffirmed the conversation that emanated from the online networks, sending the hashtag back through the boundary from the real to the virtual.

The reaffirmation stage unfolds in two ways. Primarily, it is a matter of Black Twitter participants reusing the hashtags to discuss ongoing issues that they relate to the initial discourse—conversations that have transcended the online boundary and often been discussed in physical settings, such as when friends get together for dinner, or even in conference panels, as #SolidarityIsForWhiteWomen was in the years after its creation. Secondarily, within personal communities and neighborhoods, the reaffirmation step is facilitated by both the reuse of the hashtags as well as the retweeing of information that cites the initial hashtag as part of the physical-world discussion. This process gives legacy status to some of the key markers of the cultural conversation that takes place online. Arguably, whenever the #SolidarityIsForWhiteWomen hashtag is referenced, individuals who are familiar with it as a cultural artifact will know of its significance because of both Twitter-based conversations and real-world reaction to it.

Reaffirmation is a necessary step that separates the symbolic discourse of the Black Twitter network from everyday chatter among a group of connected Black users of Twitter, leading the way for vindication through for conversations that yield tangible outcomes in the real world.

ACHIEVING VINDICATION VIA SOCIAL CHANGE

Black Twitter's discourse is concerned with championing the beauty, power, and value of Black life first to ourselves and then—often incidentally rather than intentionally—to the world around us via private-in-public conversation. This is vindication, the last stage of Black Digital Resistance: as our narratives counter the mediated constructions of who we are, changes take place in the world away from the keyboard. Both culture and technology make vindication a complex process that crosses multiple spheres of influence. One form of vindication taken up by Black Twitter confronts white supremacy in the instances where Black thought and cultural production is delegitimized through misrepresentations in news coverage, political rhetoric, and other forms of public discourse. Carter G. Woodson, founder of Negro History Week (now extended and formalized as Black History Month) explained race vindication as intellectual labor undertaken "to prevent [Black people] from becoming a negligible factor in the thought of the world" (Woodson 1926). A second form of vindication unfolds within Black Twitter's personal communities and neighborhoods and focuses on the internalized nature of white dominance in the form of intragroup sexism, queer and transphobia, and the silencing/squashing of voices that emanate from outside of elite spaces. For the sake of clarity, I'll refer to this form of self-advocacy within the race as justification, a means of reconciling Blackness as a state of being with many variations therein.

Uplifting the Race via Digital Counternarratives

Race vindication is evidenced by cases of interest convergence between Black folks and corporate, white-centric media, and is part of a long

tradition of public thinking and writing undertaken by individuals attempting to uplift and encourage the race throughout history. Historians
V. P. Franklin and Bettye Collier-Thomas put such labor of Black intel-
ligentsia into context in a 1996 issue of the *Journal of Negro History*,
wherein they recall the work of Black public intellectuals who were
motivated by a set of political commitments that are the antecedents
to Black Digital Resistance: "belief in distinct and positive African
group traits, the consciousness of shared oppression at the hands of
whites, the awareness of mutual duties and responsibilities of African
peoples to each other, and the need for black self-determination and
solidarity" (Franklin and Coller-Thomas 1996). Further, Franklin and
Collier-Thomas described the individuals committed to race vindication as "African-American preachers, professors, publishers, and other
highly educated professionals put their intellect and training in service
to 'the race' to deconstruct the discursive structures erected in science,
medicine, the law, and historical discourse to uphold the mental and
cultural inferiority of African peoples."

#OscarsSoWhite is an example of race vindication via Black Twitter's
cultural connectivity and online conversations. Although the hashtag
began in true Black Twitter fashion—as a pithy joke aimed at calling out
Hollywood's routine dismissal of talent among Black people and folks
of color—its strategic use within the Black Girl Nerds neighborhood
and subsequent amplification in Black digital media spaces arguably led
to some symbolic (if short-lived) changes in the entertainment industry. In 2015, April Reign was an attorney who often live-tweeted along
with members of the BlackGirlNerds.com online community. Using
the hashtag #BGNLiveTweets, the group would sync Netflix accounts
and watch 1980s-era movies and TV shows "together," live-tweeting
the action in the same way Black Twitter watched live television shows
like *Scandal* and *Game of Thrones*. While watching TV in her home
one morning, Reign noticed that all of the nominees for acting were
white and fired off a single tweet: "#OscarsSoWhite they asked to touch
my hair."

One year later, the slate was again devoid of any representation of people of color, and Reign joined forces with other members of the #BGNLiveTweets group to stage an online protest. As they simulcast *Vampire in Brooklyn* during the Oscars broadcast, users in the Black Girl Nerds neighborhood tweeted #OscarsSoWhite to lodge their complaint about whitewashing in Hollywood. The hashtag had immediate traction in part because of the sheer number of participants and tweets. In the months prior to the #OscarsSoWhite organized protest dozens, if not hundreds, of users used the hashtag to establish rapport with one another and to amplify Reign's message to others in the BlackGirlsNerds community—including users who either worked in or produced media. These latter users included podcasters Rod and Karen of *The Black Guy Who Tips*, who by virtue of their audiences were able to spread awareness about the hashtag. By the following year, when the Academy once again nominated a nearly all-white slate of nominees, the hashtag had gained enough attention to cross over into mainstream media coverage. Within months, the Academy announced its intentions to diversify its ranks, tipping off a series of similar changes in Hollywood and vindicating those within Black Twitter who had used #OscarsSoWhite to call out anti-Black erasure in the first place.

The collective action of individuals in the Twittersphere to advance a cause of importance to a primarily Black personal community or Black-centric Twitter neighborhood is evidence that they find vindication within the network. The ties and sense of community fostered and felt by my collaborators is real—confirmed by individuals' willingness to take action in the physical world based on information shared and relationships formed in the digital world. This phenomenon was evident during 2013, an era frequently mentioned in some of my earliest interviews (which I refer to as the Summer of Accountability) as being indicative of Black Twitter's sense of community. Multiple episodes that summer, which are discussed in later chapters, reflected the Afrocentric principles of kujichagulia (to speak for ourselves) and ujima (collective work and responsibility).

Justification as Vindication

Now, folks who consider themselves part of Black Twitter might say it's not that serious—sometimes we're just getting our jokes off, sometimes we're just calling racism out by its rightful name. But attention must be paid to the form and forum of this part of the process of Black Digital Resistance, as the ability to transcend boundaries of time, space, and place are also essential tools in fighting internalized anti-Blackness when it appears as other forms of oppression. For example, the race men and women whose names and works are part of the canon in analog Black studies and Black history have all managed to see their work published, received, and debated among the masses by virtue of class mobility—even as Black thought was (and is) being routinely discounted by white power structures. A prescriptive focus on "Black excellence," rather than an embrace of Black sufficiency, is proof of this truth.

For the rest of us, vindication within Black Twitter is a matter of justification—a process of contending with internalized anti-Blackness, which takes on rhizomatic properties within our communities, manifesting as classism, sexism, colorism, tribalism (i.e., the Diaspora Wars), queerphobia and transphobia, and other forms of self-stratification that threaten our cohesion.

> My platonic life partner @_____—she talked to me about sexuality. It was so refreshing to be able to seek information and be able to talk to people. For so long, I associated queerness with whiteness. My family is working-class with middle-class aspirations. My concept of queerness It was so refreshing to be able to seek information and be able to talk to people. It was safer online: *"There's a person in NY, maybe I can be friends with them, hang out with them."* When I think about how many straight friends I have, that list is not long.
>
> I was also figuring out myself, and I realize that now. Having the opportunity to figure myself in these created safe spaces was instrumental. Twitter created these spaces like that in 2011, 2012. The safe spaces, the welcoming spaces, the collective spaces were made online (@dopegirlfresh, 2020).

@dopegirlfresh's experience on Twitter reflects points of intersectional erasure that occur when Blackness focuses too much on whiteness and the white gaze, the other edge of the sword in Black Digital Resistance; and indeed, in many spaces where racial justice and reconciliation have been the goal. The tension of needing to be aware of white supremacy and how it operates, and recognizing our own potential for complicity in creating structures that extend oppression via silencing and erasure also played out within Black Twitter's conversations and the culture that they produced.

In addition to our discussions and hashtags and memes that contend with white supremacy from the periphery of Black collectivity, access to the platform also allowed many more individuals outside of well-accepted and long-established centers of power such as universities, government, entertainment, and media to contribute to the discourse about Black life. Further, it gave folks an opportunity to contribute to those conversations without many of the (community-imposed) strictures that police such speech when folks on the margins are invited into spaces governed by the politics of respectability. The voices of poor Black folks, queer and trans Black folks, Black immigrants, Black women, and individuals who were all of these things at once and more are heard and amplified in spaces and ways that their unknown and unnamed predecessors—Black people who were agitating alongside more well-recognized names, like DuBois and Wells, but whose narratives have been largely lost to history—never were. John Hope Franklin may well have been speaking about those whose voices rise from the margins of elite Black culture within Black Twitter to call our attention to the ways Black folks repeat patterns of essentializing our own existence. He said, "the writing of history reflects the interests, predilections, and even prejudices of a given generation. This means that at the present time there is an urgent need to re-examine our past in terms of our present outlook" (Franklin 1963). Even as our conversations with one another created evidence that countered white supremacist narratives of Black life, collectives of Black folks used "the master's tools" of segregation and subordination inside our communities, because we've internalized what it means to be Black in a way that confuses uplifting the race with meeting external definitions of who we are. Thus the insights of those who come to Twitter and aren't college-educated, middle-class, wealthy, Christian, Western, cisgender, or defined by any other "respectable" measure of Blackness compel Black Twitter to consider how we position Black life to the exclusion of some of our own people, particularly Black women.

3

Black Women's Work

It was like a scene ripped straight from a Shonda Rhimes script: a Senate race, charged with scandal, could tip the balance of power between the country's executive and legislative branches of government. If news media headlines were to be believed, the fate of our republic rested squarely in the hands of Alabama voters on December 12, 2017. The seat, long held by Republicans, was in political play for the first time in twenty-five years following Jeff Sessions's confirmation as US Attorney General. Coverage of the race focused on racial lines: the GOP candidate was backed by white, working-class voters—and the sitting president, Donald J. Trump. The Democratic nominee, a relative unknown to most of the country, had the support of African American voters in the buckle of the Black Belt.

One year, one month, and eleven days after former secretary of state Hillary Clinton won the popular vote yet lost the presidential election, progressives across the country were looking to Alabama to send a message to Washington and to the rest of the country. When the polls closed at 7 p.m. news coverage kicked into high gear, breaking down why—despite allegations that the GOP nominee, Roy Moore, had preyed on teenage girls forty years prior—either candidate could win. Precinct results were reported on the hour, every hour, and in smaller increments where time permitted. Having learned from the 2016 presidential election that anything is possible in a post-Obama era, millions of Americans stayed up through the night, watching to see how it would all turn out.

I went to bed.

I knew that if there were one voting bloc that could be counted on to act in the interest of untold scores of disempowered groups by voting as a means of self-preservation, it was Black women. And the political conversations on my own Twitter timeline about the election reassured me that if Black women in the heart of Dixie could overcome voter suppression, they could be counted on to herald a resounding rebuke of the populist politics that had characterized the 2016 election.

And Black women delivered.

kiki's anxiety service (here less often!) @kdc Dec. 12, 2017 ⋯
Like I don't think that people get that Black women don't turn out because of some maternal instinct to save everyone. We usually get hit first and worst by oppressive policies, so we are saving ourselves. You just benefit.

▶   ◯   577   ⟲   11.2 K   ♡   50.7 K   ⬆

The next day, Twitter was alight with the hashtag #BlackWomen as millions of users talked about the role Black women voters played in the Alabama Senate race, as exit polls indicated 98 percent of them voted for Doug Jones. The hashtag became a digital artifact that reflected how Black Twitter's community connections and networked communicative practices have influenced social media discourse, particularly the meta-network's ability to render our power visible. Context was offered, as in the tweet by @kdc that gave perspective about our voting-as-harm-mitigation strategies. Juxtapositions between Black women voters and their white women counterparts were raised as another attempt at white-balancing, demonstrating the differences in where and how we choose ourselves while a majority of white women who voted in the 2016 election cast their ballots against the interests of women's citizenship with all the rights and privileges thereof—not to deny it to themselves, but to see it denied to others as a means of control. Conversations both on-line and in physical spaces were held to talk about the implications of the election. Slogans were launched. T-shirts were printed. Jones would lose the seat almost as quickly as he'd won it, falling to a retired college football coach in the 2020 election.

For many Black women, and people who study Black women through a Black feminist lens, the outcome of the 2017 Senate race in Alabama was somewhat predictable. As Patricia Hill Collins theorized nearly thirty years ago in her pioneering work *Black Feminist Thought* (1990), the collective standpoint of Black women's knowledge and advocacy can be reliably called upon to work in the interest of social justice for members of our in-group. But, as I detail in this chapter, it is also a lever for others disenfranchised by normative systems of oppression—including the law, economic policy, and media practices. An examination of how Black women use Twitter reveals that we often use the platform for collective engagement in theory building and the development of critical praxis. Through ongoing conversations among personal communities and thematic nodes committed to social justice and the empowerment of Black women and girls, the women of Black Twitter live out the truth in one of the Combahee River Collective's statement of beliefs, that "our politics evolve from a healthy love for ourselves, our sisters and our community which allows us to continue our struggle and work" (1977).

Black women's ongoing engagement in Black Digital Resistance online allows us to reframe public narratives. Through our social media use, we develop both individual and collective strategies for survival by confronting the social construction of reality as it is shaped via the social construction of news. In this chapter I look at several examples, primarily from 2013 to 2017 (with a little reach in each direction of the timeline), to argue that Black women have used Twitter to amplify the impact of our personal and thematic community connections, seizing upon culturally resonant cues to reshape the social construction of Black mediated reality. From calling out the forces that impinge upon Black motherhood, to identifying how white feminism still fails to value the cognitive and material contributions of Black women, to tracing emergent theoretical developments by Black women intellectuals on Twitter, the women of Black Twitter have carved out a series of spaces for the development of emergent theory that speaks to our experiences. Online, we learn more about ourselves and each other, supplementing formal education that rarely values Black women as the philosophers and strategists these online interactions reveal us to be.

In her book *Beyond Respectability: The Intellectual Thought of Race Women*, Brittney Cooper focuses on the spaces in which Black women become public intellectuals who are concerned with all aspects of Black being. Situating Black women's intellectual labor in time and space, Cooper argues that "we must begin to look for (Black women's) thinking in unexpected places, to expect its incursions in genres like autobiography, novels, news stories, medical records, organizational histories, public speeches, and diary entries" (2017, 12). Could there be a more unexpected place to observe and trace Black women's thinking than a platform like Twitter, or a more complex arena than the interstitial space of Black Twitter? I also address Cooper's call for Black women scholars to advance the work of Black feminist theorists from the pre- and early internet eras into the digital age. When she asks, "What, for instance, is a Black feminist account of freedom? What is a Black feminist account of justice? What is a Black feminist account of Black life?" (p. 17), I look to Black women's use of social networking platforms like Twitter to actively dispute the dominant narratives about our existence, forging misogynoir's twin evils—sexism and racism—into a publicly accessible compound lens through which the white racial frame is made plain to anyone who bothers to look or listen.

I argue that the digital discursive practices of Black Twitter's actors across a series of both high-profile incidents and everyday, banal conversations represent a strategic negotiation of access, technological affordances, media literacy, and cultural competency in the creation of Black counternarratives. Black Twitter allows ordinary (read: outside of the media elite) Black people to serve as gatekeepers for the news and information needs of a plurality of Black American experiences— with perspectives not found elsewhere. This process is particularly meaningful to Black women, who continue to do battle with pervasive mischaracterizations of our beings and beliefs. While we are not the only ones to do so, Black women have used Twitter to create a series of collaboratively constructed counterfactuals, which invoke decades—if not centuries—of collective knowledge about how our experiences differ from what is considered "the norm."

From our ability to drive diversity conversations in entertainment, to our influence on political processes (both heeded and ignored), the women of Black Twitter are responsible for the creation of social media messaging that offers a perspective that centers race and gender as a more dynamic way of seeing the world. In this sense, Black women's participation in Black Digital Resistance is also part of a longer legacy of telling the detailed stories that mainstream news media refuses to see and acknowledge. And it's not for a lack of trying. Carla Murphy's research on "the leavers" (2020) highlighted how Black women make up the largest group exiting the journalism profession among people of color, even though we have been part of the work of Black public counternarrative creation nearly as long as Black news media has existed.

In their expansive survey of how race historically shaped American news media, Juan González and Joseph Torres noted that some of the earliest Black publishers printed news about Black communities while dealing with the tensions of living and owning a business before the Civil War (2012). Samuel Cornish and John Russwurm committed themselves to the cause of Black counternarratives at the expense of pushing for abolition because of the ever-present threat of white surveillance and violence (O'Kelly 1982). But some of the foremothers of Black journalism used the pen to call for resistance to the subjugation of slavery and demand more decisive action as part of their program of racial uplift. The work of Mary Ann Shadd Cary, a contemporary of Frederick Douglass, is an example of what literature scholar Tamika Carey refers to as Black women's "rhetorical impatience" (2020). Cary urged her brethren to "do more and talk less" on issues of abolition in the years before the Civil War. Ida B. Wells-Barnett's campaign to combat the memory hole around lynching in the South is well-documented by authors including Paula Giddings (2001), while Industrial Age journalists such as Maria Coles Perkins Lawton advocated for the elimination of the Associated Press' use of openly derogatory language in reference to Black people (Smith and Phelps 1992). Her work serves as a precursor to the late twentieth and early twenty-first-century campaign to have the same wire service capitalize the B in Black when used as a noun to describe us as a culturally specific group. From Lucille Bluford, the first Black woman initially accepted into the nation's oldest journalism graduate program at the University of Missouri in 1937 (Loupe 1989), to Char-layne Hunter-Gault (2012), who earned a journalism degree after being one of the first two Black students admitted to the University of Georgia in 1961, Black women's labor has been essential in the ongoing struggle for accuracy, fairness, and truth-telling in media narratives about Black life.

WHY FOCUS ON BLACK WOMEN?

Black women in the United States are subject to a litany of control-ling images about who we are and how we exist. Research by Jerald, Cole, Ward, and Avery (2017) suggests that the cognitive energy re-quired to deal with mediated stereotypes has negative consequences that impact our long-term health, an assertion media scholar and medical anthropologist Moya Bailey has taken up in her expansive monograph *Misogynoir Transformed: Black Women's Digital Resistance* (2021). Bai-ley explores several concepts of Black women's being—including who is named as a Black woman, femme, or womxn—describing the work that these sisters do across platforms as "digital alchemy." This chapter is a complement to that work, detailing Black Digital Resistance as a process born out of Black women's specific uses of and gratifications ob-tained by being a part of Black Twitter. Recognizing that Black women are surrounded by "misogynoir," a term Bailey coined that aptly de-scribes the intersection of racialized hatred targeting Black women, the collaborators who contributed to this chapter indicated a keen aware-ness of how the world sees us through the lens of controlling images like the Mammy, the Jezebel, and the Sapphire, as well as newer itera-tions including the Welfare Queen, the Hoochie Mama, the Hood Rat, and the Gold Digger. They collectively confessed that indeed, navigat-ing these warped depictions of our lives is draining, but the communities we've created for ourselves within Black Twitter's meta-network can and sometimes do provide a sense of support for balancing the stressors of navigating both online and offline mischaracterizations.

In a departure from the "shifting" that Black women often do to manage social and emotional capital in our relationships, the women of Black Twitter engage in intensely personal online, hypervisible social media discussion about the realities of coping with sexist and anti-Black stereotypes. Whether tweeting from locked or public accounts, whether with thousands of followers or just a few dozen, my collaborators described navigating the platform in a way that allowed them to perpetually be in the company of Black women. Specifically, they referred to other Black women who can both relate and join us in navigating these challenges. Our quotidian conversations become discursive acts of resistance in our refusal to be "defined against dominant notions of White femininity and the characteristics that we are hegemonically presumed not to have: innocence, beauty, worth, and virtue" (Griffin 2012b, 147). But as one of my earliest collaborators, @jus_JNC, pointed out, the digital hush harbors of Black Twitter still fail to provide a sense of respite from the social policing of Black women's lives and bodies:

> Any topic related to what Black women can and cannot do, Black Twitter has something to say about it. When I say anything, I mean *anything*. Weave, short hair, long hair, educated, if we have kids, don't have kids, too many kids, too short, too tall, too fat. Black women are always a topic of discussion on Black Twitter. I wish I knew why. I laugh and tell myself If people could walk in our shoes. We're damned if we do and damned if we don't. I think I'm more aware because of the criticism I see that Black women take. It's only since I've been on Twitter that I realized that people critique us so much and so harshly. Other Black women, Black men, white women and people of other ethnicities.

Like another collaborator, @yemisi, @just_JNC said she still turned to Twitter for perspective because it was one of the first places she learned about Black feminism. Then a student at the conservative, predominately white Liberty University in Lynchburg, Virginia, @yemisi described seeking connection with Black Twitter from the moment she opened her eyes each day:

> I have an iPhone, so as soon as I wake up, the first thing I do is get on my phone and get on the Twitter app. I really never get on the computer and get on Twitter. Whenever there's a pause in life, I get on Twitter. If I'm not doing anything, I get on my phone and I'm scrolling through my TL. On my TL, Black Feminism is a big deal. My little cove of Black Twitter. I didn't really know about the issues that Black feminists deal with that white feminists don't have to deal with. From my TL, that's really important.

The platform equips us with the ability to make our knowledge production public and shared, contributing directly to the culture as it exists online. On Twitter, we grapple with the sexual scripts that render our own girlhoods in liminal states of hypersexualization. We juxtapose media frames of Black mothers with white ones to resist erasure and abjection. Day by day, we work out a series of responsive practices that help us mobilize against the destruction of Black bodies, Black people, and Black communities.

I have a particular interest in this work as it is pursued by Black women because Black Twitter is one of the few spaces where our intellectual work can be easily accessed, and is thus often exploited, without the benefit of its knowledge being applied to foster justice in the world. Online, our knowledge production flows without the disruption of having to accommodate the white racial frame, which Joe Feagin describes as a schema combining beliefs, cognition, affect and actions that affirm and uplift whites while devaluing and negating or erasing Black people and "others" through a series of frames and subframes (2013). The invisible influence of the white racial frame characterizes mediated news and information as being produced with a "view from nowhere," whereas scholars including McIntosh (2018), DiAngelo (2018), Painter (2010), and Feagin himself (2013) have pointed out that the social construction of whiteness (and its inherent privileges) is considered to be the default existence. Whiteness maintains its hegemonic influence, these scholars suggest, by presenting the world "as things are" instead of interrogating public values and norms as the outcome of a complex set of historically defined power relations. Through our lived experiences, Black women are compelled to confront these power relations on a daily basis, and our conversations often reflect the strategies we have developed to negotiate them successfully, and to interpret the world from our relative positions of power.

Twitter helped render these discursive processes visible to the masses. The platform's broadcast dynamic, as Clay Shirky observed, positions conversations through a "many to many" model, allowing for a plurality of speakers to address a multiplicity of audiences all at once (2008). Black women used it to develop spaces for online conversation that highlight our perspectives at the intersections of race, gender, and class—theorizing in ways that center our vulnerabilities in the pursuit of justice beginning with speech acts and scaling up to structural change. In "the digital beauty salon," as Catherine Knight Steele calls our online spaces, Black women create culturally resonant hashtags and less-visible conversations that signal the complexity of our experiences (2016). Speaking from our various corners of the world, we put our knowledge into the ephemeral, esoteric digital atmosphere and use it to affect our concrete, offline experiences.

Through our culturally resonant conversations on Twitter, Black women's writing moves us and our intellectual products "from margin to center," positioning our lived experiences as the compounding lens for intersectional media analysis influenced by degrees of "otherness."

Developing Critical Counterfactuals as a Form of Digital Counternarratives

Black women's theorizing tends to occur in collaborative spaces—kitchen tables, the workplace, sorority meetings, beauty salons, or lesbian reading groups. As the literary scholar Barbara Christian wrote, Black women's intellectual labor is more interested in fluid rather than fixed ideas; as we are often grappling with ever-changing dynamics of domination and subjection (1987). It's a process of creation that we undertake on a daily basis—devising concepts, models, and explanations for the way the world works, the way it *should* work, and the way it actually works for us.

The theorizing that arises out of Black Twitter's everyday conversations is intricate and grounded in common experiences. Some of the easily indexed examples of this process are the embedded meanings in high-profile hashtags such as #BlackGirlMagic, used to point out our creative power; #FastTailGirls, which confronted the hypersexualization of Black girls; #YourSlipIsShowing, created by Shafiqa Hudson (@sassycrass) to point out trolls posing as Black feminists on the platform. The stories communicated through these hashtags, as part of the affirmation and reaffirmation process of Black Digital Resistance, are complex enough to reflect a range of Black women's experiences, while being cohesive enough to persistently move forward with the intention of achieving social justice goals based on the demands of the times. The hashtags are indicators of dynamic narratives that link Black women's experiences across time, place, and status, developing strategies for survival and thriving. Yet the theorizing that occurs among Black women on Twitter cannot be limited to the written word. It begins with the embodied experience: the historically bound situated knowledge each participant brings to the platform.

Black Twitter's online conversations and theory building often rely on a compound of creative counterfactual and situational juxtaposition that have been used consistently over time to bring the white racial frame into focus, pointing out how normative assumptions of being are predicated on the affordances of whiteness, and leave Black folks out of the equation. The strategies allow social media users to collectively illustrate white supremacy's subliminal machinations, a process that educator and activist DeRay McKesson signals when he tweets "watch Whiteness work."

CONSTRUCTING CRITICAL COUNTERFACTUALS
One early example of Black Twitter's critical counterfactuals was the community's response to Casey Anthony's acquittal for the murder of

her two-year old daughter. Like the rest of the country, we'd watched the case unfold on broadcast and cable news and followed the updates on social media. But when the jury returned a not-guilty verdict in July of that year, Anthony's storyline quickly took on a new dimension. Historian Imani Perry reflected on the comparisons Black Twitter made in a column for the *Miami New Times*, an alternative weekly:

> I read tweet after tweet with the following formulations: Had Casey Anthony been a Black woman, she would have been convicted. And while Black women are being jailed for sending their children to good schools, white women who murder children are let off.
>
> The fact is, we cannot say what would have happened had the race of the actors been different . . . a different case would have simply been different. (2011)

The issue at hand, Perry went on to note, was about racial inequity in the criminal justice system. I read the subtext a bit differently. Not only was Black Twitter reacting to the documented disparities in punishment between white and Black defendants, we were using the comparisons to draw attention to the public's lack of sympathy to the plight of Black mothers.

Danielle Fuentes Morgan, an African American literature scholar, notes that "the protection implicit in motherhood is overwhelmed by social structures that refuse to allow the Black body the space to exist autonomously. Black women, and Black mothers in particular, are familiar with this fact in theory and in practice even as it is denied in American publics" (2018, 859). She continued: "Motherhood is pithily cherished in the mainstream popular imagination, yet Black motherhood historically has not been afforded these sorts of shields."

Just six months before Casey Anthony was brought to trial, Kelley Williams-Bolar, a mother of two in Akron, Ohio, had been sentenced to jail and restitution for lying after using her father's address to send her daughters to a better school in the neighboring district (Rose 2013). Williams-Bolar's case highlighted the complexities of Black motherhood—how redlining and education policy, for instance, intertwine to create a second-class experience for Black Americans who want the same opportunities for their children. According to an ABC News story, "school officials said she was cheating because her daughters received a quality education without paying taxes to fund it," admonishing: "Those dollars need to stay home with *our* students" (2011). The response reflects a position firmly affixed within the imaginary lines of tax districts drawn around white suburbs in the decades following federally mandated school desegregation. That same year, Tanya McDowell, a homeless Black woman in Bridgeport, Connecticut, enrolled her five-year-old son in a school outside of her district and was ultimately sentenced to time in jail for her actions, alongside a conviction of drug trafficking.

The comparisons between Anthony, Williams-Bolar, and McDowell are not about the letter of the law and the presupposition of guilt, though those are the grounds on which they are introduced. Black Twitter used these incidents to construct counterfactuals that takes aim at dominant depictions of Black motherhood.

In mainstream media coverage, the Black mother is a cousin to Reagan's welfare queen; the horror of Moynihan's single-parent matriarch brought to life. Legal scholar Dorothy Roberts, in her 1997 article "Unshackling Black Motherhood," traces the degradation of Black maternal figures from the era of slavery, with descriptions of Black women's purported "ease" in childbearing, to the 1990s, when hospital toxicology records were sampled to portray impoverished Black mothers as the public scourge birthing so-called crack babies. Roberts raised and critiqued three strategies to decriminalize Black motherhood: telling the whole story, telling details about Black women's lives, and highlighting the abuse of Black women's bodies. These narrative techniques can be observed in Black Twitter's discourse about Black motherhood. They invoke not only race and gender to highlight differences in power dynamics, but also call up details of the lives of Black women at the center of these stories and share their own, to provide adequate context for rationalizing an otherwise criminalized course of action.

Holding the storylines of Black mothers invested in their children's survival parallel to a white mother's alleged involvement in the murder of her own child creates a dramatic counternarrative that allows Black intellectuals to engage in social critique that mainstream media is unprepared to compose. By parsing the details of each case—how poverty presents Black families with limited options for advancement, how education remains the ticket to class mobility, how the enforcement of arbitrary boundaries like school districts acts as another tool to control Black potential—users illustrate the forces that complicate Black mothers' abilities to care for their children. They reveal the processes complicit in criminalizing Black motherhood. Such comparisons continued as late as 2019, when news broke of Operation Varsity Blues, a federal operation that broke up an elite college admissions scandal. Some of Black Twitter's key voices evoked collective memory of Williams-Bolar's experience to highlight how race, gender, and class create a different set of circumstances of acceptable parenting for Black mothers. Their observations were reaffirmed outside of Twitter by Black women with more traditional platforms, including Ashley Alese Edwards of Refinery29. Edwards discussed these narratives in a column about the admissions scandal: "In a system that already favors the rich, moms like McDowell face few other options in trying to secure quality education for their children" (2019). Jenn M. Jackson, an assistant professor of political science at Syracuse University and contributor to *Teen Vogue*, echoed her sentiments: "When parents of marginalized, poor students try to navigate around the harsh rules and requirements, they are often investigated, tried, and punished with strict prejudice," she said. "The entire system is corrupt, biased, and unjust, leaving poor Black and brown students the least protected" (2019).

As Black Twitter knows, exposing the long-tailed effects of systemic oppression is a difficult and complex task. The abstractions constructed within these counterfactuals tease out the peculiarities of American social systems that allow colorblind racists to couch their critiques of Black people in the letter of the law. Critiques that rest on the assumption that the law is a rational process, blind to the identity markers of Black skin and social class, and impervious to the historical record of how these markers influenced earlier eras. The social media users who layer these seemingly dissimilar experiences over one another are pointing out the differences of *justice*—not legality, since we can point to a lengthy history of legal codes and statutes that enabled the injustices of slavery, segregation, and now, mass incarceration. Black Twitter's counterfactuals identify the infrastructure that frames Black deviancy in news media, and subsequently in public consciousness. They are crafted again and again, striking upon glaring differences that illustrate how a potent mix of internalized bias, racial myths, stereotyping, and media framing subjugates Black existence.

A Different Perspective

These constructions rely on a number of factors. At least two people— one Black, and one white—are cast in the lead roles. Occasionally a non-Black person with closer proximity to whiteness (i.e., white Hispanics or light-skinned Asians) fulfills the latter role. No matter their background, the antagonist must be the evident beneficiary of the privileges outlined in sociologist Peggy McIntosh's discussion of the invisible knapsack—the unearned, unquestioned privileges conferred by white identity, even among poor whites (1988). Their whiteness, or proximity to whiteness, affords them a different experience than one a Black person would likely have. Like Anthony, Ethan Couch (the Texas teenager who killed four people and injured nine others while driving drunk) and other white people who seemingly escape punishment for their real or perceived misdeeds, this character benefits from a series of social checks that affirm whiteness as a preferred position, and Blackness as an undesired, unfortunate one.

Blackness, the interlocutors of the imagined scenario presume, invokes a different set of character and moral judgments, triggering negative frames in the minds of authority figures with power over Black subjects. These assumptions aren't wholly imagined—studies on the perception of Black children indicate that non-Black people often view them as older than they are, and for whatever reason, inscribe their bodies with adult characteristics. So too do studies of the perception of Black patients by doctors—that we're somehow less impervious to pain, and thus undeserving of the timely relief medical interventions can provide. Colorism, as a proxy for class, also informs these assumptions. Research on Black girls in public schools suggests that darker-skin girls are subject to harsher punishment than girls with light skin, a troubling indicator that has also been tracked in algorithmic predictors of recidivism, once thought to be a tool for creating more equitable sentencing determinations for potential parolees. The history of surveillance and the physical policing of Black bodies—Black existence—gives counterfactual contributors a wealth of raw material to draw on for constructing schema of disadvantage and maltreatment on the basis of race.

Thus such ideas shift the locus of understanding about how one's actions might be influenced by their race rather than the "objective" details of the case. The US approach to reporting—a key contributor to the social construction of reality by which the law, public decorum, and shared mores are all laid upon—emphasizes the latter, which are not so much "objective" as observable and quantifiable. Such details are thus defensible under the law, the primary control mechanism of the Fourth Estate. Reporting that emphasizes the ability to draw upon these documentable realities is critical for the news industry to tell a story quickly and as accurately as it deems possible, historical context notwithstanding. News media's failure to engage in critical examination that includes a power analysis of intersecting oppressions leaves individuals in the lower domains of the Matrix of Domination to fend for themselves. This creates an explanatory void that other individuals in similar positions must fill through incisive reasoning, and must then communicate to others in the most effective way we know how—through the use of story.

Which is how we come to the seemingly incongruent comparisons of culpability between a mother accused of murder and mothers accused of taking advantage of public funding. The conversationalists within Black Twitter who make these comparisons have a different frame of reference for developing the story narratives that influence each case. They rely on the dynamics of power to identify differences in what is considered fair, normal, just, and, most of all, expected, by centering the history of power and its influence that leads each character to their chosen course of action, and each player and observer in the story to their own perception of an objective truth. This approach to sense-making of everyday phenomena presents a completely different set of frames for individuals who are otherwise judged by the narratives of the dominant culture.

For instance, a consideration of the history leading to the Black mothers' choices to send their children "outside" of their district forces audiences to walk through the abuses of power that brought each to a moment of moral reckoning. Using the history of Black existence to contextualize modern phenomena, the audience must consider how the residual effects of domination—beginning with enslavement and the denial of literacy, evolving into segregation and underfunding to desta-bilize social progress, and culminating in white flight and redlining to control access to resources—might lead a Black mother to "transgress" invisible boundaries of belonging to grab hold of the promise of educa-tion for her children. By way of moral relevance, and an ethical reasoning that the ends justify the means, Williams-Bolar's actions were sympa-thetic, as were McDowell's. To what end should a mother be faulted for seeking a better education, or immediate financial stability for her chil-dren? Rotating the argument to its axis of race and gender dynamics exposes the circumstances that frame popular assumptions about Black motherhood: the absentee Black father myth characterized Williams-Bolar's plight, even though, in keeping with research that indicates Black fathers are equally involved in their girls' lives with their non-Black counterparts, the girls' father was implicated in the case. It was *his* ad-dress that allowed her to enroll the girls in a better school. The 1980s-era urban legend of crack babies as a drain on public resources was re-vived through a focus on McDowell's involvement with drug trafficking. Add to these perspectives the struggle to avoid the trappings of poverty, wherein others decide that your children are not "our children" and thus unworthy of a quality education, despite both parents being tax-paying citizens, and these mothers' choices become part of a larger, more complex story of Black resistance to subjugation. It's a story few in mainstream media have time or perspective, or motivation to tell. Yet to Black Twitter's participants, it's an important account that bears out the differences Black people—in this case, Black mothers—are up against each day. And so the story must be told. It *is* told—by drawing upon the power of collective memory, shared experience, culturally resonant semiotics, and metaphor to weave the narrative over time through a series of tweets.

Such abstractions are repeated every day within conversations among Black Twitter's participants. They were constructed on matters of race and police brutality when users compared the treatment of Dylann Roof with that of Stephon Clark. Roof, a known fugitive who massacred nine worshippers at a Charleston-area AME church in 2015, was arrested without incident and given a fast-food meal while in pretrial detention (Ray 2022). Clark was an unarmed Black man gunned down with a phone in his hand, after emergency callers reported a Black man breaking car windows in the Bay Area (Lipscomb et al 2019). They invoke the name of Joshua Williams, a Ferguson-area activist sentenced to eight years in jail for property damage (Stewart 2016). By comparison, Brock Turner, a Stanford student athlete, was sentenced to a mere six months—and then released early—after sexually assaulting an unconscious woman (Chappell 2016; Brand 2022). By comparing these stories on the basis of race and class, and using evocative imagery to bring the history of discriminatory treatment applied through laws, rules, and contemporary norms, Black Twitter seeks to draw attention to the ways that these identity markers carry exponentially significant weight in tipping the scales of justice.

As both women *and* people of color, Black women are particularly compelled to engage in the creation of counterfactuals to make visible the powerful influences in our lives that aren't readily reflected in news media. When a notion of "objectivity" characterizes the information-gathering and sense-making processes of newswork, it has little ability to consider the prism of human experience, particularly how power dynamics built on the construct of race shape esoteric yet venerated concepts like justice. There are countless additional examples. The limits of motherhood as a defensive position for Black women was a subtext to the #FreeMarissa campaign on Twitter from 2015 to 2018. Marissa Alexander, mother of three—including a newborn daughter—was sentenced to three years in jail and two years of home confinement in 2013 for firing a single shot in the garage door of her Jacksonville, Florida, home (Montgomery 2013). She fired the gun, her defense team argued, as a warning shot to deter her abusive partner from lashing out again. Alexander's case was argued on Florida's so-called Stand Your Ground statute, under which George Zimmerman, the white Hispanic man who fatally shot sixteen-year-old Trayvon Martin, was acquitted of murder in 2012. But Alexander was convicted under the state's 10–20–Life law, a gun control measure enacted in 1999 by tough-on-crime conservatives to target gang activities. While Alexander and Zimmerman's stories were compared up until the time she was freed from home confinement in 2017, the narrative around her conviction remains in circulation as part of a Black Twitter counterfactual comparison: white men and women brandish guns and evade similar punishment, or even death, unlike the scores of unarmed victims memorialized via hashtags during the height of the Movement for Black Lives. We extend these comparisons to other instances of physical and psychic violence committed against Black people when white people are not subject to similar treatment.

These comparisons have certainly predated Twitter and other forms of digital media. Ida B. Wells's Red Record, a detailed history of the lynchings of Black people in the United States that went unreported by the Justice Department, springs to mind as a striking antecedent, a volume through the broken bodies of Black people served as testament of the different concepts of "justice" as defined by race. If not for her decision to bear witness to the atrocities committed in the spirit of maintaining an American public committed to the ideal of "law and order," we would have fewer points of reference by which to measure the degree of difference race confers in matters of the law and social expectation. The Black American history of storytelling as a means of documenting racial injustice is a backdrop to the digital counternarratives that Black Twitter creates today.

Social media forces users outside of Black communities (where the platforms' algorithms allow them to see such conversations) to grapple with the history of these incidents and compels non-Black people and those with a shallow concept of truth to consider alternative perspectives of incidents in which the immediate, observable facts alone do not convey the whole truth of the matter. The public construction of counterfactuals imports engagement of the racialized imagination and compels onlookers to reconcile factors of race, gender, class, and other identity markers that influence the way Black people experience the world. The tools equip users to bring Black hieroglyphics to life through the use of memes, videos, and audio components, and set our stories on a collision course with narratives of the dominant public sphere.

And when we invoke our shared knowledge of how such scenarios would play out if the Black aggrieved were instead white with a simple "you know why" on Twitter, the verbalization receives a visual assist through the platform's affordances. The ability to combine text and images contributes to the iterative formation of digital counternarratives that link together disparate instances of Black folks' mistreatment with a finite summation of multiple examples—from the inability to tell two different Black people apart, to the way justice and punishment seem to have different rules of engagement for those of us in Black skin.

"You know why" is rarely a matter of simply comparing group means; it highlights the ways Blackness infuses our lives and experiences with a range of difference. But the controlling forces remain the same. And so does the moral of the story: Black existence is costly, complicated, and can be deadly.

In addition to serving as key contributors to these counterfactuals, Black women on Twitter emerged as powerful agents of knowledge through our network connections, shared culture, and ongoing conversations. Through algorithms, surveillance, and our word of mouth, our cultural knowledge production on Twitter was translated into valuable resources for a number of groups. These groups include writers who have co-opted ideas and conversations for their own articles, often without attribution, but also organizers seeking to educate and mobilize divergent publics about the issues that unite them, as with the #BlackLivesMatter movement. Whether debating the merits of Olivia Pope's professional and sexual agency in #Scandal, reveling in the messiness of Mona Scott-Young's *Love & Hip Hop* reality television shows, collectively grieving with sisters memorialized by #SayHerName, challenging our white counterparts to recognize the shortcomings of White Feminism, calling one another out on the stratification of Black womanhood along lines of class and gender expression, affirming our own beauty when one of our stars has been written off as "less classically beautiful" or with more casually racist references to her hair skin or dress, the women of Black Twitter engage in forms of narrative theorizing that are responsive, adaptive, and of semiotic significance across media ecologies that have systematically erased our work.

Our existence as agents of knowledge is not linked solely to the "both/and" nature of being Black women, but by our lack of proximity to social capital and structural power that makes the intellectual exercises of Black women—throughout media history—critical to reshaping public discourse, and through it, a more just social construction of reality. The "both/and" nature of Black women's existence is a metaphysical prism for understanding the world from a position of vulnerability. In our online conversations, we use that perspective to symbolically dismantle media systems designed to retain hierarchical systems that keep the least among us from being robustly and compassionately understood as valuable human beings. For years, Black women on Twitter took up this world-(re)making work by pointing out the structural inequalities that defined our lives, describing the various ways we worked and are working through them, and suggesting new ways of seeing the world.

Talking Back: The Stuff of #BlackGirlMagic

The news media's tendency to erase the structural elements that minimize Black Americans' equal participation in our society aren't limited to traditional publishing venues. When CaShawn Thompson, a native of Marion Berry's DC, tweeted #BlackGirlsAreMagic, she provided a resonant summation of Black women's alchemy. Affixed with a hashtag, it was truncated as #BlackGirlMagic, and has since served as shorthand for Black women's panache—our ability to endure the bilateral cruelties of racism and sexism and emerge with our humanity fully intact, and to do so with an embodied style all our own. Sociologically, it's a call-up of one feature of Collins's *Black Feminist Thought*—the dynamic ability to adapt and thrive in any context; artistically, it's a call back to Maya Angelou's *Phenomenal Woman*, crunched into fifteen characters and easily affixed to selfies, testimonial tweets, and celebratory posts heralding Black women's achievement. Like other theoretical signals, its arguments have been introduced, developed, adapted, and challenged within intellectual communities—ones that exist outside of the academy and thus freed from its legacy tax, but with a politic of citation that warrants both popular and scholarly recognition.

Themes from dominant narratives that feign concern about the demise of the Black family would otherwise frame Thompson as a one-dimensional figure: a teenage single mother who once lived in poverty. Such characterizations are endemic to analyses of family structures that do not match the white racial frame—a nuclear family with a white, married, monogamous, cis-gendered, heterosexual mother and father and their progeny. But Thompson, through her years of lived experience being a Black girl and then raising Black children, produced a cultural label that does the work of neatly and succinctly describing Black girls' abilities to survive the hardships we face from cradle to grave.

When a user affixes #BlackGirlMagic to a tweet commending the newest crop of Black women graduating from college or basking in the glow of our own melanated beauty, they are signaling an understanding of the complexities these women had to navigate to make it to a particular moment of self-actualization and normative achievement. #BlackGirlMagic, as Thompson defines it, is a call-out to Black women's empowerment. It is a narrative device that through three simple words and an indexable hashtag, serves to strengthen in-group affirmation and out-group recognition as Black women reclaim our identities and sense of self. After centuries of laboring under the derogatory yet normative frames assigned to us, which Rachel Alicia Griffin bemoaned in her Black feminist autoethnography reclaiming the "Angry Black Woman" (2012b), invoking #BlackGirlMagic gives Black women intellectuals a device for pithy redirection, rejecting the hackneyed tropes of the mammy, the Jezebel, the Sapphire, and their contemporaries—the

Hoochie Mama, the Hood Rat, the Welfare Queen, and the Gold Digger. Still, the #BlackGirlMagic label isn't a simple antidote for the deviant
frames that plague public comprehension of what it means to be as a
Black woman or girl. The label has been subject to ongoing criticism, as
Linda Chavers proclaimed in her hotly debated 2016 essay "Here's My
Problem with #BlackGirlMagic," published by *Elle Magazine* online. A
subheading clarified: "Black girls aren't magical, we're human." #Black-
GirlMagic, Chavers argued, should not be codified as a sentiment to
mask the entrenched structural, political, and economic forces Black
women contend with, often at physical and social cost.

> The "strong, black woman" archetype, which also includes the mourn-
> ing black woman who suffers in silence, is the idea that we can
> survive it all, that we can withstand it. That we are, in fact, super-
> human . . . Black girl magic sounds to me like just another way of
> saying the same thing, and it is smothering and stunting. It is, above
> all, constricting rather than freeing. Black girl magic suggests we are,
> again, something other than *human*. That might sound nitpicky, but
> it's not nitpicky when we are still being treated as subhuman.

Chavers positioned her own experience living with multiple sclerosis as
an example of how use of the phrase had potentially damaging effects,
with the potential to erase the work it was crafted to do—highlighting
the extraordinariness of Black women as equal contenders in a fight for
humanity.

Separately, the phrase has been critiqued in its use to signal
respectability—that only a certain kind of achievement is "magical," and
it often fits into preconstructed notions of what Black excellence looks
like according to the white gaze, or, at best, the Black middle-class point
of view. In this sense, the co-optation #BlackGirlMagic turns a phrase
intended to indicate our ability to thrive into a digital cultural product
shaped by hegemonic standards of capitalism, individualism, and assimilation. Without considering the intention and perspective of its creator,
#BlackGirlMagic can be exploited in ways that limit our understanding
of Black achievement to terms of our ability to satisfy white normative
value judgments.

Yet Black women on Twitter resist this oversimplification each day in our online conversations, and through the critical praxis that develops from them. Working through our networks of personal communities and developing Black digital enclaves hidden in plain sight, we have engaged in these digital resistance practices to confront, interrogate, and challenge mainstream media tropes of Black womanhood. Dayna Chatman did this in her 2017 exploration of the online conversation around the premiere of *Scandal* in Season 3, when the lead character's affair with the president is exposed. Distinguishing fans from anti-fans and using Henry Jenkins's concept of the fan (one who creates out of love for a particular cultural artifact or performance), Chatman drew attention to the way Black women engaged in dialogue about the politics of respectability, the burden of representation, and the rejection of tired tropes about Black womanhood and Black sexuality. This fan discussion, according to Chatman, created an online forum where Black female representation was made and remade, echoing Stuart Hall's observation about Black popular culture—that it is a dynamic space where identities are continuously contested (1993). Additional examples can be found in our reaction to the mainstream media gaffes that indicate (non-Black) people can't tell Black women apart, or that denigrate our appearance and call it cultural criticism (#lessconventionallybeautiful), or that attempt to erase the work of Black women who have advocated for our communities for years.

This work is never-ending, though we have seen it fulfill some of our goals to have the full experience of Black womanhood be recognized. The narrative theorizing we engage in on Twitter is a necessity in creating sufficient space for Black women and girls to thrive despite mediated depictions of us as deviant and unworthy creatures.

A Timeline of Critical Resistance Praxis

No one would accuse Bay Area rapper Too $hort of being a feminist. His work is the epitome of what C. Delores Tucker warned us about during her campaign to end so-called gangsta rap (Conway 2015): it's the West Coast answer to the hustle culture of New York and the nasty-as-he-wanna-be Miami bass music made infamous by Luther Campbell. All of which, I should say, I will gladly shake my Black feminist behind to. In public.

But in 2012, Too $hort recorded a video of "fatherly advice" to young men for *Complex Magazine*, essentially teaching school-age boys the art of pimping. Black feminists on Twitter, many of whom also identify as hip-hop heads or even hip-hop feminists, were not having it.

> One [hashtag conversation] I was thinking about recently was what happened after [rapper] Too Short's comments about 12-year-old girls. He made some comment about teaching middle-school boys about how to turn out [sexually exploit] middle-school girls. It sparked a really useful conversation about violence and sexual assault and harassment among Black girls. (@GraceIsHuman, 2013)

The last case I'll detail as an example of this work's critical function makes, in my estimation, one of the clearest connections between on-line discussion and the development of critical praxis. In 2013, Mikki Kendall and Jamie Nesbitt Golden, two Chicago-based writers, hosted an online conversation using the hashtag #FastTailGirls to draw atten-tion to the cultural and systemic hypersexualization of Black girls. The hashtag refers to a colloquialism that polices Black girls' bodies and behaviors—often long before they reach an age of physical, intellectual, and sexual maturity. Where the politics of Black respectability required the type of abstinence that neutralizes a range of sensual and sexual ges-tures or behaviors, Black mothers, grandmothers, and aunties sought to protect their family names and girls who wore them by labeling any re-motely coquettish behavior as "fast"—an all-encompassing euphemism used to describe everything from the physical evidence of puberty to any sense of sexual agency (Crooks et al 2023).

Kendall and Nesbitt Golden, cocreators of the blog Hood Feminism, realized thousands of other women with Black Twitter had a stake in shaping public discourse about sexual exploitation of Black women and girls into a lens for analysis where Black communities could reconsider the many ways that our own cultural norms make us susceptible to sex-ual violence. Such conversations are the link between reports of the high incidence rate of sexual abuse among Black women and girls—the National Center on Violence in the Black Community estimates that one in four Black girls will be the victim of sexual assault before they turn eighteen, and that one in five Black women are survivors of rape—and the individualized experiences that are used to develop survival tactics.

"When I first decided to have it," @karnythia said, "we were having one of those interminable 'what girls should do' conversations . . . and I thought we should talk about the idea that girls should do _____ to earn respect. We've had those conversations, me and some friends."

Labeling a woman or girl "fast" absolves Black men and boys of a responsibility to respect Black women's bodies as our own sites of representation—rather than sites of male subjectivity. It performs double duty by simultaneously shaming Black women and girls along two planes: the physical—our possession of pronounced curves, dressing in ways deemed inappropriate, acting and speaking in ways that reflect even a hint of worldly knowledge—and the cultural—the invisible weight of having to constantly check our dress and behavior against historical frames dating back to the exploitation of Sarah Baartman in the eighteenth century. To be fast-tailed is a combination of knowing what you have and using it in a way that suits you—an unacceptable choice for Black femmes, constantly monitored, scrutinized, and critiqued as representations of our communities—not just ourselves. Girls who date too early are fast. Teenage mothers are fast. Bawdy women serving body—whether fictitious, like Shug Avery, or historical, like blues women and glamour gals including Josephine Baker—are fast. So, too, are their progeny: artists and rappers like Trina, Rihanna, Nikki Minaj, and Beyoncé.

As a precursor to the online iteration of the #MeToo movement, #fast-tailgirls created a sense of visibility for survivors of sexual abuse in Black communities, and it laid some of the groundwork to bring R. Kelly into accountability. While some of Black Twitter celebrated when the R&B singer was indicted on sexual battery charges in late February 2019, a different contingent took a cautious approach to the judicial proceedings. After all, it wasn't the first time the public had seen Kelly called to account for preying on young Black girls. In 2008, he was acquitted of sexual performance with a minor after a videotape of a man said to be Kelly was submitted to Jim DeRogatis, a reporter at the *Chicago Sun Times* who had investigated the claims against the singer and found that 'no one cared about Black girls' (2019). Nonetheless, the indictment, and the online conversation around it, was (at least symbolically) incremental progress in holding men accountable for sexual exploitation of Black girls and the women they'd one day become.

As Golden told me in 2018:

> Everyone has a #fasttailedgirls story. It's ingrained in us. It started that night, we had a conversation on Twitter, I wrote the piece for XOJane, and a little while afterwards, we had the scheduled chat.
>
> Growing up, you don't realize how much we go through. There were detractors, people who said we were demonizing black men. But it was cathartic for people to know that they were not alone. You're dealing with men who are predators.

Kendall went on to say:

> We have generations of women who have been victimized. Forty to 60 percent. We have to start talking about what it means . . . That means develop ways to center Black women in conversations that touch on more widespread themes.
>
> I know a lot of people were mad white women were left out because there was this term that they didn't know that was being used with issues that they did know. I had a few people ask me about what it meant. It was one of those things that's weird to explain outside of its cultural context, and I see white women pearl-clutching around it, and I don't have time for the history lesson.

In creating a hashtag for Black women to build narratives about their own experiences, Kensall and Golden served as a space for self-disclosure and healing for a number of its participants. The hashtag remains in use as a signifier of the complicated and often cold realities of being seen as a hypersexual being before one is physically, mentally, or emotionally sexually mature. It has resurfaced most recently with the *Surviving R. Kelly* documentary produced by dream hampton.

"I now know that if you get on Twitter and you give people permission to speak with a hashtag, they will unclench. The well of their souls will pour out. I have seen people confess their lives online, publicly," Kendall told me. Several years after that fateful night, the call-out of cultural practices that position Black women and girls for exploitation resurfaced in Taranna Burke's #MeToo, a hashtag that, like #Solidarity-IsForWhiteWomen, tapped into similarities and was adopted to birth a shift in social dynamics.

MAKING THE INVISIBLE, VISIBLE

Our voices are finally being heard when they make visible the hardships and oppressions we face at the intersections of race, gender, class, ability, and access. And our struggles for justice—first in our own communities, then radiating outward—have found a useful tool in the net's abilities to bring our physical networks closer together. Whether we are Black mothers, knowledge workers, writers, or everyday women emblematic of the social vulnerabilities of Black women and girls who lacked sufficient standing in mainstream media narratives to be constructed as worthy victims, Twitter gave us a common gathering place to deliberate these issues with greater attentiveness to their complexity.

Day in and day out, Black Americans on Twitter have engaged in the difficult work of making racial subjugation visible in the media and pointed out the myriad ways media's reach impacts Black communities. As researchers have observed:

> Much of what comes to pass as important is based often on the stories produced and disseminated by media institutions. Much of what audiences know and care about is based on the images, symbols, and narratives in radio, television, film, music, and other media. How individuals construct their social identities, how they come to understand what it means to be male, female, black, white, Asian, Latino, Native American—even rural or urban—is shaped by commodified texts produced by media for audiences that are increasingly segmented by the social constructions of race and gender. Media, in short, are central to what ultimately come to represent our social realities. (Brooks & Hébert 2006)

Black women, whose existence is precariously stretched inside of these constructions, have a particular interest in making the media's role in the devaluation of Black life plain. While foremothers including Anna Julia Cooper, Ida B. Wells, and others had the limited resources of the printing press to educate wider publics about the precarity of Black life, modern activists have the exponential influence of digital media connected via social media, which allows them to create complex, multimedia counternarratives of Black lived experiences and circulate them alongside traditional texts.

Via Twitter's technological tools and Black Twitter's cultural and sociolinguistic ties, the women of Black Twitter have been uniquely situated to engage in a form of theorizing that acutely informs critical praxis in making our lived experiences, and the invisible influences of power that runs along the lines of race, gender, and class, visible and tangible to others in our communities and people outside of them. While our representation in mainstream news and entertainment media continues to lag, our formation of communities of practice and communities of thought on social media have amplified our voices and our influence on how the world sees us in ways our foremothers could not have seen.

There is perhaps no greater example of the power of this phenomenon than the emergence of the largest racial justice movement in the digital age, brought to life via hashtags and headlines through the initial work of three Black women—Black Lives Matter.

4

Agency, Activism, and Agenda-Setting

5'7 Black male @absurdistwords 37m
Chants of "social media doesn't matter" ring hollow and false as hashtags become movements become household words

▶   30   ↻   16   ♥   49   ...

5'7 Black male @absurdistwords 36m
We are standing in the middle of a lot of history.
Dead center, where the world shifts course again.

▶   30   ↻   22   ♥   63   ...

I was sitting in my apartment on Saturday, August 9, reviewing slides for my dissertation defense when I saw the first hashtagged mentions of #MichaelBrown on Twitter. I didn't have a television at the time, so Twitter was my primary source of news and information. Based on the tweets it was difficult to tell what had happened, but a few key facts were clear: a police officer had shot and killed a Black teenager outside of St. Louis (Shoichet 2014). His body was still in the street. A crowd was gathering, with smartphone cameras trained on the scene, relaying updates via text and multiple social networking platforms. I clicked away from my slideshow presentation and over to CNN.com to find out more about what was unfolding in Ferguson, Missouri.

Less than one month after witnessing cell phone video of Eric Garner being wrestled to a New York sidewalk and seeing the life literally choked out of him, Black Twitter had become conditioned to seeing hashtag memorials pop up on our timelines and begin to trend as people posted information about incidents of white violence that claimed Black lives. As #Ferguson, #MikeBrown, #MichaelBrown, and #BlackLivesMatter began to trend, I was also troubled by how the news media was covering Brown's slaying and the resulting protests in Ferguson. Analysis of news coverage from that era indicates that the headlines and stories about the Ferguson Uprising followed the protest paradigm, with frames that delegitimized protestors' actions before judicial pronouncements—such as the failure to indict Brown's killer—were rendered, and only delving into the ideas that informed the protests after the killers walked free (Brown et al. 2019). Instead, stories reported out of Ferguson were hyperfocused on property damage and destruction—easily quantifiable metrics devoid of human context that offered gripping images and news hooks. On Twitter, though, we found connection with people from Ferguson who provided real-time accounts of what life was like when tanks drove through their neighborhood and previously empty corners were occupied by police armed with military-grade weapons. The juxtaposition of these two narratives underscored the necessity of Black Digital Resistance as a means of troubling public perceptions about Black lives under siege. What Black Twitter provided was commonality: as I did more than a year earlier when Trayvon Martin's killer was acquitted, I heard echoes of my own devastation in the words of those who posted their raw, agonized thoughts of the terror ripping through Black communities yet again. While the news media scrambled to piece together the story, their reports did not—could not—adequately reflect the sentiment of what lay beneath our hashtagged memorials and tweeted grief.

This chapter considers how the process of Black Digital Resistance reinforced Black Twitter's participants' sense of agency, enabling them to participate in networked activism and to articulate emerging standards for care of our communities. By examining agency, activism, and agenda-setting during the initial wave of the Movement for Black Lives, we can better understand why Twitter served as such an effective platform for amplifying concerns from diverse Black communities, even when their messages were sometimes distorted. This chapter focuses on the interplay between news media framing of Black grief and grievance, and Black Twitter's response to both those frames and the incidents they attempted to narrate for the imagined audience. The limits of news reporting are predicated on the news worker's ability to recognize a definite action—a shooting, a protest, an indictment (or lack thereof). Walter Lippmann's observation about the function of the press exposes this tautology: "News does not separate itself from the ocean of possible truth . . . News is not a mirror of social conditions, but the report of an aspect that has obtruded itself" (Lippmann 1922). US news values are not designed to engage empathic storytelling, the kind that might consider the conditions through which people are forced into certain neighborhoods, or the attitudes they might develop as a result of constant surveillance and the imperceptible but certain threat that because you are Black, your life may be in danger at any time. While reporters descending on Ferguson could publish stories about property damage and loss, estimates of the number of people in the streets, and even detailed histories of how years of overpolicing and the devaluation of homes in the area have extracted value from the St. Louis suburb, they could not adequately describe how the death of another Black boy reverberated through the lives of Black people across the country—or throughout the world. Black Twitter provided a glimpse across the ocean of possible truths from Black perspectives in the wake of Brown's death—and every other name hashtagged and memorialized as was his. Despair. Rage. Fear. These are conditions that are unquantifiable, but present nonetheless.

This is not new news. Mistrust of news media within Black communities is informed by its historic failures to faithfully and fairly report on the lives of Black people. It is a systemic issue that has been charted in every form of Black media-making since the publication of *Freedom's Journal* in 1827, though each generation of mainstream news media covers the reaction to these disparities as though they are novel responses to episodic events. From *Freedom's Journal* pushback on the homogenization of Black culture in the early 1800s to Ida B. Wells's *Red Record* compiled between 1892 and 1895, white-owned mainstream papers either ignored, commodified, or vilified Black people in the United States, a practice that allowed white readers and leaders alike to spin their own narratives about Black communities, with lasting consequences. As the Industrial Revolution shifted social classes, formerly nonwhite immigrants and poor white Americans found themselves begrudgingly welcomed into the narrative fold of whiteness as foils for Black laborers seeking better economic opportunities via the Great Migration. Black news outlets, from word of mouth via Pullman Porters and newspapers like the *Chicago Defender* and the *New Amsterdam News*, helped circulate printed instances of useful information to Black communities along migration routes. As discussed in Chapter 1, Black media production—such as the Black press's coverage of the civil rights movement (Grimes 2005)—has been a consistent avenue for resistance in the struggle for liberation, even when ownership of the technologies used to create that media is structured by white normative practices and beliefs.

Black Twitter's responses to Brown's death, and to the dozens of names hashtagged in memorial, is a dynamic demonstration of how social media users who otherwise felt disempowered in the face of unrelenting, caught-on-video assaults and slayings responded to both the anti-Black violence itself and the news media as an apparatus upholding the normative values of the state: "People can fight only in the arenas open to them with the tools they have" (Lipsitz 2011).

TWITTER USE AS A MEANS OF EXERCISING AGENCY

@Rick_NYC had followed another case of anti-Black police violence for weeks. Shocked and sickened as he and millions of others witnessed replays of Garner's 6-foot-4, 300-pound body being pinned to the pavement outside a Staten Island convenience store (Sanburn 2014), he threw himself into researching police and judicial procedures of censuring officers accused of misconduct.

"Finding out that the chokehold was an illegal chokehold, I had hope," he explained. "You see it, we've got footage. I thought to myself, this might be the case."

The medical examiner's initial report, which listed homicide as the cause of death, seemed to support that judgment. @Rick_NYC thought that the incontrovertible video evidence of a Black man's life being snuffed out, crushed below several officers as he gasped and pleaded "I can't breathe!" would be sufficient to invoke a penalty: an indictment and conviction on charges of murder or even manslaughter—anything that formally recognized the theft of a human life. It wasn't. A Staten Island grand jury refused to indict twenty-nine-year-old New York police officer Eric Pantaleo in the chokehold death of Eric Garner, forty-three (Siff, Millman & Dienst 2014).

"I work with about three other Black people, and we had to privately be hurt," @Rick_NYC said. He and his Black coworkers gathered in an empty room to check in with one another after the decision was announced that afternoon, but they had to disband quickly. As the day wound down, @Rick_NYC turned to Twitter for both solace and a plan of action.

> I did not know where the protests were going to be. I did not know what website to go onto. I typed in #EricGarner; I wouldn't have known where to find it. We're at 23rd and Broadway, we're making our way to the Brooklyn Bridge. We crossed the bridge, the juvenile detention facility. It was amazing to be around those people chanting. I would not have been able to do that without Twitter. I felt connected, and I felt at ease. I could have gone home and been emotional, been angry at a situation. But to be able to go on Twitter and find these people . . . I was not with any friends. I went out there and ran into someone I knew and said "I didn't know you were going!" she said, "I didn't know you were going either."

The meeting of two friends in the middle of a protest was anything but serendipitous. On the contrary, the encounter confirms the efficacy loop that vindicated hundreds of thousands of people using Twitter to connect via their calls for racial justice during the first wave of the Movement for Black Lives.

They may not have known it at the time, but hundreds of people who took to the streets in cities across the United States protesting the verdict in Garner's case in December 2014 were assisted by a woman in Michigan. In 2014, Leslie MacFadyen (@lesliemac) created the Ferguson

Response Network as a Tumblr site where she compiled and posted details about protests and marches. Speaking to my Black Digital Culture class in 2017, she recalled developing the idea to construct the Blackchannel after working with another Black woman she'd never met but had often talked to on Twitter.

"There was a woman in New York named Feminista Jones who organized the National Moment of Silence, and I reached out to see if I could help her," MacFadyen told me. On August 14, 2014, five days after Michael Brown was slain in Ferguson, Jones organized a synchronous international vigil using the hashtag #NMOS14 (National Moment of Silence 2014), in large part to extend a space for grieving for New Yorkers who couldn't make it to midtown that Sunday for a public ceremony. At 7 p.m. Eastern Standard Time, participants around the world stopped to collectively grieve Brown, Garner, and the untold numbers of Black people whose lives had been cut down by racialized violence. With a following that at the time numbered in the tens of thousands, Jones had the reach to promote the hashtag. MacFadyen provided organizational assistance by collecting information about community-based vigils scheduled for the #NMOS14, creating the precursor to the Ferguson Response Network Tumblr. By the end of 2014, the site had hundreds of posts about activist networking tools, including information on meetings and protests in more than forty states and six countries. It has since become an archive of sorts, with most of the fliers and bills that were posted by other Tumblr users removed from the site.

I first spoke with @LeslieMac in 2015, a year after the initial Ferguson Uprising. At the time she was still heavily involved in racial justice organizing, an extension of the criminal justice reform work she'd been a part of when #MikeBrown began to trend in 2014. She recalled the conversation that moved her work from outside the church and into the larger networks of protest:

> I had been put into a task force by my faith—I'm a Unitarian Universalist—on August 9 of last year. We were people all around the country who were already concerned with what was going on in Ferguson and trying to get patched into UUs in the St. Louis area.

We put together this curriculum for clergy to be able to talk about what was happening in Ferguson in their sermons, around religious education, and some talking points for the press with clergy in our faith. We started meeting every other day or so, and we formed some subcommittees—people working on religious education, the media kit, and some working on sermons. And really making sure we were telling the right story, that we were framing things well.

It's a predominately white religion, so we really wanted to make sure we were ahead of whatever misinformation might be out there. So out of that, I got in touch with a bunch of clergy in St. Louis. A couple of weeks before the grand jury decision, they were doing de-escalation training, preparing for whatever the outcome was going to be.

I threw this question out there: "What do you want other people to be doing? What should we be doing outside of Ferguson?" And they were like "we don't even have the bandwidth to think about that right now."

It was a lightbulb moment to me within the movement, and what it means to me: "If you think that something needs to be done, then do it." It's a very powerful moment, and that's why the movement has caught on in such a strong way. When you see people changing their lives and adjusting what they do, because there really is this empowerment level to it.

That realization was @LeslieMac's catalyst toward participating in the hashtag activism surrounding Ferguson, and more broadly, the online activity indexed by #BlackLivesMatter. Her relationship to the protests is a reflection of Black Digital Resistance at work: @LeslieMac's self-identification as a Black Jamaican woman raised in New York is part of the subtext, signaled by her acknowledgment that the UU church is "predominately white." She self-selected into the process of Black Digital Resistance through her commitment to online organizing, which crossed platforms from Tumblr to Twitter throughout the first wave of the protest movement. @LeslieMac's lightbulb moment about movement work via social media is—like Rick's decision to channel his emotions into the action of street protest—an indicator of the sense of agency being a part of Black Twitter bestowed to hundreds of thousands of people using the site to draw attention to injustice during the first wave of the movement. That awareness transcends basic self-efficacy when users translate their feelings into action, whether by tweeting along with hashtags about racial justice, adding their voices to cacophonous conversations about cases like Garner's, or pushing back against media narratives that deny Black folks equality in personhood.

More extensively than the way the Facebook page "We Are All Khaled Said" served as a coordinating site among networked individuals contributing to protests during the Arab Spring (Alaimo, 2015), the Ferguson Response Network Tumblr became one of many tools essential to a loosely defined network's ability to meet, inform, and organize itself in the service of civil disobedience. As Rainie and Wellman discuss in their book *Networked* (2012b), the "triple revolution" of increased internet access, proliferation of mobile phone usage, and social network connectivity assisted by social media platforms provided critical assistance in helping ordinary people like @Rick_NYC take on a more activist role, even if their direct engagement was limited. But a hyperfocus on the social media component of contemporary social movements often obscures the social and cultural ties that bind Black users to one another in between the moments that bring Black Twitter's meta-network into light.

The practices that linked @FeministaJones, @LeslieMac, and @Rick_NYC together in this moment connect the synthesis between Black Twitter's tri-leveled networked structure and its participants' engagement in discursive practices of resistance, particularly the affirmation, reaffirmation, and vindication stages of Black Digital Resistance. As #EricGarner trended that night, similarly themed neighborhoods within Black Twitter were linked together by users like @Rick_NYC, who located information about protests and other forms of direct action. The tweets and retweets that linked online conversations and offline mobilization allowed users to affirm one another's emotions, and to have their own outrage and despair reaffirmed by moving out into the street, as @Rick_NYC did. This gave users an ability to see, hear and touch the embodiment of briefly linked, briefly unified Black communities who found collective courage in the face of oppression.

A brief explication of the online affirmation process is essential in order to understand the significance and scope of digital activism and micro-activism among Black Twitter users. The number of individuals who mobilized to engage in traditionally recognized forms of activism—marching, boycotting, and other physically-oriented protests—was a fraction of those who strategically tweeted hashtag memorials and images attesting to anti-Black violence. For instance, when a white police officer forced fifteen-year-old Dajerria Becton (NBC Dallas-Fort Worth 2018)—clad only in a bikini—to the ground and knelt on her back during a pool party in McKinney, Texas, few ventured out to stage protests in the Dallas suburb. But #McKinney and #BlackLivesMatter trended that day and for several days after as people discussed the heartbreak of seeing another Black child assaulted by police. As a hashtag, #Black-LivesMatter helped maintain these connections as episodes of racialized violence were caught on cell phone video and broadcast both online and via television and radio. In addition to stepping away from work meetings for a respite from the chaos outside, people within Black Twitter were able to turn to their online networks. They recognized themselves, their friends, and their families in the faces of individuals like Korryn Gaines (Knezevich & Rector 2016), Chikesia Clemons (Harris 2019), and Ahmaud Arbery (Fausset 2020). Through each use of the hashtag, they participated in a range of discussions about whiteness, policing, and Black life, and found affirmation that their perspectives were being heard if not shared by others like them online. Reaffirmation came in the form of finding further connection in offline activities. Tynes, Schueske, and Noble (2016) discuss this digital intersectionality with regard to marches like the one @Rick_NYC and his friend participated in, as well as sit-ins and die-ins publicized online. Black Twitter found vindication in Black Digital Resistance in much the same way other needs are satisfied—first through small changes like hearing the language of our struggles spoken openly, and then larger ones, like seeing the moral arc of justice bend in our direction as more people began to identify with the racial justice aims of hashtagged protests such as #SayHerName and #MeToo.

The tri-tier network of Black Twitter plays an important role in the process through which every day users found agency in our digital activism. The individuals who make up Black Twitter, including their tiny personal communities, became hubs and spokes in the ephemerally linked neighborhoods that formed around specific themes—not just police reform and abolition, but also reproductive justice, education reform, and anti-capitalism. Within these clusters, and through the meta-network of Black Twitter that came into focus each time a name became a hashtag, the process of identification, self-selection, participation, affirmation, and reaffirmation helped Black Twitter connect and comfort one another as its networks decried racialized violence and other forms of mistreatment.

Over the years, we've experienced a number of outcomes that can be qualified as "vindication"—though to be clear, vindication is not a finite state of being. The conviction of Arbery's killers is an example of this: in light of guilty verdicts for the three white men who effectively lynched their neighbor, many Black users posted confessions that peace was still elusive. Discomfort unsettled the abolitionists among us, who could not cheer for the carceral state finally deciding that its measures were warranted for white people, too. And those of us who, like me, struggle to escape carceral logics found fleeting satisfaction in the guilty verdicts. For a moment, yes, these convictions served as "vindication" that our efforts to draw attention to racialized violence did not return void—but only as long as the decisions were held up on appeal. Justice, as I tweeted the day Arbery's killers were convicted, would mean having Ahmaud still with us—that however his run began that day, it would end with him safely at home (Fausset 2020). Even today, as his killers petition the courts for preferable treatment, we are reminded that the project of Black Digital Resistance is part of the ongoing struggle for Black liberation, simply described in technological terms.

FROM AGENCY TO ACTIVISM

Researchers have given years of study to questions about motivations for tweeting with social justice and racial justice hashtags. They have combed through datasets comprising millions of tweets to make sense of how and why Twitter users select that particular platform to air their grievances, connect, organize, and mobilize. After three years of interviewing folks who identify as part of Black Twitter, I'd grown more interested in the granularity of such online activity. Who were the people behind the accounts? Why did they use Twitter to draw attention to crimes against Black people? And what, ultimately, did it all mean for the way we understand the concepts of agency and activism in the web 2.0 world? Within a decade, Black Twitter had developed digitally mediated processes for citizen journalism that documented assaults on and within our communities. It had also created its own rituals for collective grieving and consolation and measures for demanding public accountability from otherwise out-of-reach figures, including celebrities and politicians.

For many, the opportunity to participate in rituals of collective grief and mourning was important. Several of my collaborators spoke of using Twitter as an outlet for the anger, frustration, sadness, and despondency that grew out of repeatedly watching or hearing about Black lives being ended at the hands of white law enforcement officials. Participants repeatedly invoked the importance of the sense of community when sharing their grief via the social networking site. Whereas @Rick_NYC and a few of his Black coworkers had space to share their disappointment behind closed doors in their workplace, others found that Twitter provided the only public comfort they could find. For users like @BrookeObie, an attorney-turned-writer based in New York whom I interviewed for research on #BlackLivesMatter, Black Twitter's use of hashtag memorials was an opportunity to join into elegiac embrace for the memories of fallen fictive kin.

@me:
I want to go back to something you mentioned about the hashtag being very unifying. And I'm sorry if this seems really elementary, but when you say those hashtags have been unifying, is it specifically like the hashtag with the name of the person or justice for, let's say, Sandra Bland or Trayvon Martin? Which of those hashtags and particularly referring to?

@BrookeObie:

All of them. I think when I say unifying for one, we know their name. They're particularly as Black women who have been brutalized by the police and by men in our own community and outside of it. You know, our names get forgotten, though, hashtag like, say her name. You know, that's so powerful. Yeah. I mean, I guess it gets us on the same page. So, you know, I really appreciate that because I don't know that I would know Rekia Boyd or Renisha McBride or Sandra Bland or Ayanna Stanley Jones if not for these hashtags. Because again, when you're tweeting about this stuff, too, you're tweeting, you're retweeting your writing this name over and over and over again.

Like it's like a prayer, you know, an exercise. You know, "I'm not going to forget you." Like, "I will do what I can to remember you, to get justice for you, to make sure this doesn't happen to anybody else like that. Your death won't be in vain."

That's what I feel like every time I see that, every time I type it, that's what I get out of it.

Even to people who aren't religious, it's like we're all like praying together, like saying the same name. It's like, you know, when you're in church and everybody says, "hallelujah" at the same time, or everybody says "Jesus" at the same time. Like, it's like the same kind of thing. Like we're calling on the same power, like we're calling on the same name, like we're on the same page. We want the same thing. And irrespective of our differences between us right now, we are getting together to get this justice for this person who we understand is not just this person. Like, #SandraBland is not just Sandra Bland—she's all Black women. Like Mike Brown. It's not just #MikeBrown. He's all Black men—all Black boys—you know. So it's just this is a very . . . a great way to build community and also find people who believe like you believe.

Like @Rick_NYC, Brooke said she also participated in several marches, using Twitter to stay informed about developments following the deaths of Eric Garner, Michael Brown, and Sandra Bland (Laughland 2019). Black Twitter, she said, offered her a channel to keep up with real-time news, information and narratives untold by mainstream media, and gave her the ability to participate in BLM as a racial justice movement through a continuum of activities, from retweeting information to locating protests and marches to contributing via crowdfunding.

> In the midst of this despair, there was this silver lining of community. It was different to experience it with this community, even though we weren't physically in the same place. Twitter gave me the feeling that I could do something, I could send a donation. They had set up a fund for protestors that were down there [in Ferguson]. Being able to send money, being able to share. I don't have the largest following, but having a verified mark helps me show up higher, being able to amplify that. Feeling like I could do something even though I haven't been there. (@BrookeObie)

@BrookeObie, @Rick_NYC, @LeslieMac, and @FeministaJones's activities are in line with Marichal's (2013) concept of social media microactivism on Facebook, "politically oriented communication that reflect micro-level expressive political performances." While individual Black Twitter performances (a term I also use to describe part of the process of Black Digital Resistance) may not be consistently geared toward scalable intervention such as group mobilization or resource-sharing, they allow individuals to perform their "would-be selves." They shape both individual and communal-level social identities of the world as it might be if those in the Black Digital Resistance were structurally positioned or equipped with more political power. Marichal's concept identifies expressivity, identity, signifiers, and length as four dimensions of expressive equipment on Facebook. Applying this concept to Black Twitter requires additional consideration of the critical factors that compel users to voice their positions and concerns on the microblogging platform in the first place. Brevity replaces length, and the signifiers, rather than being coded in strictly political/partisan terms, are linked to ethnic, racial, cultural and gendered existence. Expressivity is made all the more urgent by the perceived potential for amplification. Identity, though, becomes the most multifaceted of the affordances. On Twitter, the ability to suspend one's existence somewhere between "nonymous" and anonymity, while also choosing to signal group membership and cultural belonging, allows Black users a degree of dynamism we cannot enjoy in offline life, as the corporeal signifier of Blackness allows others to immediately encode us via their specific beliefs and pre-existing schema. On Twitter, we can profess and perform Black identity, but also shield our Black bodies from certain degrees of exposure—doxxing notwithstanding.

While the urgency of the movement may have been seemingly tempered in the wake and aftermath of the 2016 election, and its push for racial justice temporarily revived with the addition of more names to the ongoing list of hashtag memorials, there is more to Black Twitter than the work of making invisible audiences of color more recognizable to mainstream media executives, and situating Black death as a catalyst for civic change. Their discussions, indexed by the creative hashtags that made Black Twitter a recognized phenomenon beyond its own boundaries, are evidence of how the network(s) created its own counter narratives that briefly disrupted the same sort of news coverage that the Kerner Commission warned about a generation before.

In many of my collaborators' memories, protests in Ferguson and New York overlap as the offline events which drew their attention to the #BlackLivesMatter hashtag. Participation in protest via Twitter was often the only way to connect with like-minded individuals outside their immediate communities. Several participants spoke of being physically house-bound, and thus unable to travel to and participate in marches organized throughout the country. Others referenced limitations of time and physical distance as obstacles to joining protest efforts on the ground. But years before #BlackLivesMatter made Black struggle against the state salient for the digitized masses, smaller protests, spearheaded by pockets of death-penalty opponents across the country, linked together. They formed blueprints for the neighborhoods of Black Twitter's denizens and friends who would eventually take to the streets. For many who could not or chose not to mobilize in terms of street protest, or who were not as closely connected to the meta-network of Black Twitter, seeing narratives about Black lives, and watching moments of Black death, catalyzed a reaction to news media coverage of Black life in America, prompting an ongoing cycle of reactions to troubling coverage that distorted the truth about our existence.

THE AGENDA-DISRUPTING POTENTIAL OF BLACK DIGITAL RESISTANCE

In the nearly fifty years since the Kerner Commission report warned of the country moving toward "two Americas: one Black and one White," and implicated both law enforcement and news media as two major players in accelerating this divide, internet technology has provided an opportunity for "the people formerly known as the audience" to collectively work out narratives that addresses critical issues of concern to Black communities. The introduction and use of social media, in particular, has been instrumental in allowing Black Americans to counter mainstream media depictions of our everyday realities. Whereas earlier iterations of Black counternarratives were often contained in Black-specific publications and cloistered in our cultural commonplaces, Black Digital Resistance evolved as networked Black protest discourses that briefly challenged mainstream media's agenda-setting function—the ability to influence both what the public thinks about and how it thinks about it (McCombs and Shaw 1972).

One particularly notable story about Brown's slaying, published in "the Paper of Record," reflects this. In a posthumous profile of the eighteen-year-old, John Eligon, a (Black) writer for the *New York Times*, recounted that he was "no angel." News stories focused on Brown's size (6'4", nearly 300 pounds), troubles in school, and a photo that some interpreted as him throwing gang signs. Black Twitter's response to Eligon's characterization of Brown offers another example of Black Digital Resistance at work: frustrated by the lack of compassion shown for Brown, one user, @CJLawrenceEsq, posted two pictures of himself with the hashtag #IfTheyGunnedMeDown. The first image, bright and light-hearted, was taken while @CJLawrenceEsq spoke at the podium during his graduation, with former President Bill Clinton laughing with other dignitaries in the background; in the second, @CJLawrenceEsq holds up a bottle of Hennesey and a mic. "Yeah, let's do that," he tweeted, indicating awareness of an aligned imagined audience: "Which photo does the media use if the police shot me down? #IfTheyGunnedMeDown." In two images and twenty-two words, @CJLawrenceEsq's tweet illustrates how racist assumptions pervade even the most routine of news gathering tasks: selecting photos to illustrate a story. Within hours, hundreds of users had joined in, posting ratchet and respectable pictures of themselves, photo-memorialized juxtapositions of Black life captured in the limited extremes of the white imagination. Their posts echoed some of the creative counterfactuals that had been expressed in earlier tweets—the burden of double-consciousness is a constant companion with Black people navigating the world.

Each pair of #IfTheyGunnedMeDown photos communicated two distinct realities: first, that news media could just as easily find unambiguously "respectable" photos of Black people if they were drawing from around the web, yet often choose—whether out of convenience, malice, indifference, or a combination thereof—images that contribute to our likenesses being coded as deviant. Second, that the use of images and hashtags together served as a cultural shibboleth for people with a common experience, who could see themselves in the face of Mike Brown and others like him as reflected in the news. #IfTheyGunnedMeDown, and later, #IfIDieInPoliceCustody (Vega 2014; Lopez 2015), a series of directives in case of the user's demise via state-sanctioned violence, helped scores of people within and watching Black Twitter recognize that they were not isolated in their concerns about news media's depictions of Blackness (Lee 2017). This affirmation of shared recognition, of hashtags created, joined, circulated and decoded, encouraged users to be mindful of what was possible offline, too. If they could share such a powerful affective connection with hundreds of users online whom they'd never met, there was space for similar connections away from the keyboard and in the streets. Indeed, in marches throughout the world, the critical nature of Black visual elements was reflected in a series of iconographic images, like the hooded selfies posted by the Miami Heat and thousands of other Twitter users, as they re-created a picture of Trayvon Martin.

WE TRIED TO TELL Y'ALL: THE NEWS IS ONLY PART OF THE STORY

Black Twitter has fashioned time-honored techniques of protest, including civil disobedience, rancorous discourse, and boycotting, and it works along the lines of connectivity to realize a sense of communal agency that echoes the striving of the civil rights movement. The "Black witnessing" from street scenes in New York, Ferguson, Baltimore, Cleveland, and other sites of anti-Black violence in the first wave of Black Lives Matter protests documented for the public "proof of the many eras of anti-Black racism in all of its perverse mutations," as Allissa Richardson has theorized in her work (2020). Between 2014 and 2016, in particular, a distinct network of Black users on Twitter emerged as effective activists for a number of causes with connections to racial justice, trading on the platform's technologies in attempt to refute the pervasive yet often latent message of white supremacy that positions Black people as something less than human.

When the practice of journalism—a central apparatus for defining and describing lived reality—is rooted in practices that categorically deny Black humanity, how then, can we as a people, engage in resistance? The strategies that emerged during the initial wave of the Movement for Black Lives are one indication of how the practices of Black Digital Resistance allowed so many to reclaim a sense of agency as they forayed through different forms of activism, much of it chronicled through their online activity linked together on Twitter. News media coverage from the time skims the surface of how Black social media users engaged in the practice of community care. This included teach-ins, creating and circulating alternative syllabi to provide the historical context missing from news coverage of the time, mourning spaces, and opportunities to channel our pride, joy, and grief into action. In addition to providing testimony via hashtags like #IfTheyGunnedMeDown and #IfIDieInPoliceCustody, Black Twitter also invoked the authority of previously published works to frame our anguish in response to the moment. Marcia

Chatelain curated the #FergusonSyllabus, a reading list and resource for teaching about the histories of lynching and other forms of anti-Black violence in the United States (Chatelain 2020). In subsequent years, her approach would be repeated within and outside of Black Twitter, as others created additional syllabi to contextualize tragedies including the Charleston Massacre (#CharlestonSyllabus), and the white supremacist march on Charlottesville, Virginia (#CharlottesvilleSyllabus). Collectively, these responses can be considered products of the wide-ranging conversations about racial justice that had been simmering in Black Twitter's online neighborhoods for years.

The individuals who use internet communication technologies such as smartphones and social networking sites such as Twitter engage in the creation of counter narratives about people on the margins—namely Black folks from a variety of economic, social, and cultural backgrounds. The "overrepresentation" of Black users on the site, coupled with the high number of journalists and their embedded cultural values, allowed Black Twitter the (sometimes unintentional) ability to both create and consume a spectrum of micro news narratives of resistance that demonstrate just how pervasive and consuming our everyday struggle against white dominance can be.

In the ongoing struggle for recognition of the fullness of our humanity, Black Twitter has served to further underscore the demand for a full-scale revolution in how US news media reports on Black people and, consequently, how the United States sees and understands Black life. If nothing else, this era of digital culture has been the culmination of the Kerner Commission report's prophetic warning to news media: that continuing in the traditions of the white media elite will lead to further disenfranchisement of all nonwhite people (particularly those who do not attempt to assimilate themselves into white culture), and eventually, the collapse of the country as we know it. While media scholars have, for at least three decades now, discussed the implications of the fractured media landscape wrought by technological advances, a cultural divide has been yawning and growing just beneath the surface of what we can see. For Generation X, millennials, and Zoomers, the disruption of the mediated world as we know it—a world constructed by traditional news narratives that our parents and grandparents lived in—was permanently severed when Black death, unfiltered by the lenses of onlookers equipped with smartphones, became a regular subject of the nightly news. It does not take news media coverage to mobilize Black folks into action. In fact, one of the reasons the protests during the Movement for Black Lives were so successful was because of the pre-existing commitments that many of us—both on and off Twitter—have to advancing Black liberation. But beyond the headlines and hashtags, Black Twitter demonstrated the necessity of using available media technologies to tell our own stories. The platform's affordances were useful for educating one another (and our onlookers) about everything from the historical underpinnings of police violence to the use of mutual aid networks that sustain our communities in times of open struggle. Most notably, Twitter allowed Black folks from all walks of life to find a central location for news about our common welfare, calls to action, and even strategies for contesting controlling images of our worth. The platform's uses in these respects was not without issue: since 2017, investigations from outlets including The Intercept, ProPublica, and the Brookings Institute have detailed how Twitter collaborated with law enforcement to track users involved in racial justice protests, and how foreign actors seized upon our online conversations to quash efforts of collective defense and confuse newcomers who entered social justice work via online channels. In April 2024, a report from the Brennan Center for Justice described how third-party surveillance companies collated data from protestors who shown up in multiple sites during the first wave of the Movement for Black Lives—and those who may not have been on site for both protests but were connected to others who may have been in Baltimore or Ferguson. But those who identified as part of Black Twitter and self-selected into conversations about the hashtagged names that populated our feeds were affirmed by finding and interacting with others who shared their concerns. Some further developed a sense of agency in watching how their online conversations made them part of a group with the ability to disrupt mainstream media narratives about Black life. And others still carried the energy of those conversations into the world beyond the screen. Through demonstrations and other forms of community care, they reaffirmed the significance of the online conversations and in some cases, won vindication by drawing attention to otherwise marginalized and ignored voices. The first iteration of this process is chronicled between 2013 and 2016, while the second wave, from 2016 to 2020, may seem less coherent. But this second wave is indebted to the initial wave of the Movement for Black Lives and its ability to make the demands of the movement salient to more people—whether they were Black or online. That in itself is a form of vindication.

What Difference Do Our Stories Make?

A year or two after I finished my PhD, I had the opportunity to return to UNC one summer as a visiting scholar in the Institute for African and African American Research. I spent the time working on a project about Black Lives Matter—specifically, the affective relationship individuals on Twitter had with the hashtag. During a presentation I gave on my project, a scholar in the back raised her hand and asked a question that essentially amounted to, "How will we know Black Lives Matter was effective as a social movement?" I believe the efficacy is embedded in Black Twitter's ability to collectively challenge and shift media narratives about reporting on Black life. This is not a finite process. To be clear, Black Digital Resistance has been met with a number of challenges, most notably the attempts to delegitimize its rationales and tactics. This is true for Black Twitter's engagement in intersectional hashtag activism (Jackson, Bailey, and Foucault-Welles 2020) and digital discourse-driven acts of reaffirmation born from the network's activities. These criticisms are launched from multiple perspectives and include negative news media framing, the disapproving commentary of venerated public figures, and rebuke from other Black people. Collectively, they can best be understood as filial tensions between generations of social actors whose approaches to understanding Blackness are bound to what Best (2018) critiques as the central quandary in Black studies: a limited definition of Black being that rests on the historical context of subjugation.

In this chapter, I have explored how Black Twitter's form and the function of Black Digital Resistance influenced a nascent period of activism in the digital age. By orienting the narrative around reactions to news coverage and uncovering links between actors using hashtags that serve as memorials and rallying cries, my interviews and observations of Black Twitter's advancement of the Movement for Black Lives offer a descriptive case study of how some Black folks' Twitter use helped them achieve a certain sense of agency during a period in which news media reports about the subjugation of Black life seemed designed to convince us we had none. After self-selecting into conversations about their experiences and their connections with the Black faces deemed as unworthy victims of white aggression, particularly at the hands of police, people like @Rick_NYC, @LeslieMac, @FeministaJones, @BrookeObie, and others found a means to cope through a number of away-from-keyboard activities, yet continued to seek connection with others via Twitter by posting, sharing, and circulating messages of support on the site. These activities included reminders of how Black people engage in white-balancing to illustrate how decades of coverage of the depravity we face, predicated on the colorline, temporarily ruptured some of the news media's ability to essentialize Black experiences. If only for a moment, this messaging disrupted news media agendas by forcing the industry to acknowledge how its disparate treatment of Black America has continued to alienate us.

As Black Twitter used the platform to call out anti-Black speech and behavior by politicians, celebrities, brands, public figures, and professors, we also used it to draw attention to troubles endemic within our bonds. We refuse to comply with the norms of "civil debate" as championed by news media and publics unfamiliar with the urgency of having their very lives and beings threatened by forces that would more willingly snuff out our lives than listen to us. That urgency underscores the way Black people respond to one another, especially in matters of rebuke and correction. We call it many things: reading, dragging, calling someone out. But in an attempt to once again crunch our existence into the white racial frame, news media gave our digital accountability discourse a new name: cancel culture.

5

From Calling Out to Cancel Culture

Black Twitter's summer of accountability in 2013—when Paula Deen, Juror B37, and white feminists everywhere were called into account via hashtags and petitions on the platform—created a precedent for how its networks of users pursued vindication for Black people both online and away from the keyboard. Whereas physical protests, strikes, boycotts, and other repertoires of contention have some, if limited, effectiveness in shifting power dynamics, it's more difficult for a group of similarly aligned—yet structurally disempowered—publics to have the same influence on nonstate actors. So when Russell Simmons announced the launch of All Def Digital, a YouTube channel featuring branded content from his label, on August 13, 2014, by tweeting a link to a tasteless parody video of the Black Moses having sex with her "massa" so as to blackmail him later, Black Twitter was forced to reckon with the media mogul using a tool we'd found effective before (just ask Paula Deen): shame.

When Simmons tweeted the #HarrietTubmanSexTape, critiques within Black Twitter focused less on the media-maker himself and more on the issues of systemic subjugation of Black women, living and dead, in both reality and fictionalized forms. Simmons's choices to reduce Tubman to a tired trope of sexual deviance incited public shaming, but also a demand for a powerful Black figure to deal with images of Black women responsibly. Black Twitter's approach toward demanding accountability in digital spaces is fashioned from our shared lived experience and sense of racial solidarity—knowing *"we all we got."* So often, as demonstrated via the hashtag memorials that characterized both waves of the Black Lives Matter movement, it is Black people who speak up for us from the safety and understanding of our own communities. This is true in cases like the #HarrietTubmanSexTape fiasco, somewhere between the gravity of calling out habitual offenders via the #MuteRKelly campaign and the laughing-through-the-pain of being systematically underestimated reflected in the mockery of a hashtag like #StayMadAbby (Walker et al, 2022), discussed later in this chapter.

The reaction to Black Twitter's use of social and digital media to call out and "cancel" prominent figures exposed the flip side of news media's tendencies to render the power within Black communities invisible. Seemingly overnight (although with a few nods to the historic notion of vocal Black folks as agitators), Black resistance via dialogue and discourse became hypervisible, and positioned as a threat to a sense of imposed order and civility. Slate magazine lumped a number of critiques emerging from Black Twitter into a glossy feature on "The Year of Outrage," (Turner et al, 2014) where one culture writer summarily dismissed the network's use of critical counterfactuals with "well, you can't argue with fiction." The writer compared the sympathy white feminists afforded Lena Dunham, who was in the spotlight over her account of an

interaction with her younger sister that was called out as child molesta-
tion, with the lack of concern shown for victims of R. Kelly, who would
later be convicted of *actual* sexual misconduct. "There is a compelling
argument to be made about how black men are criminalized while white
women are absolved," she wrote. "This isn't it."

Like every form of Black media production before it, Black Twitter has
been burdened with the task of resisting news media elites'—both individual and institutional—ability to define and determine the legitimacy
of Black critique in both substance and style. Tweets deemed as evidence
of "outrage" are in fact evidence of the harm suffered when news media collapses context around critical issues raised within and by Black
voices and communities. This form of Black Digital Resistance reaches
beyond naming and shaming. Whether Black Twitter is calling someone out or canceling them, the practice is rooted in Black vernacular
traditions, and grows out of years of being symbolically silenced in the
media spaces mythologized as part of the public sphere. Scholars Bren-
desha Tynes, Joshua Schuschke, and Safiya Noble (2016) have referred to
Black Twitter's unruly means of checking disrespect as a form of digital
intersectionality,praxis recognizing that these practices are a product
of Black Feminist Thought in the Internet Age. In the early 1990s our
foremothers observed Black women's use of print and broadcast media
as tools for communicating the alternative bodies of knowledge they'd
developed within themselves and within the corners of society we were
often relegated to. In this era, social networking platforms like Twitter
both enable outlets that span from the intimately personal, such as Black
women's blogs, to the commercial, such as *Essence* magazine, to amplify
our praxis in ways that ultimately cross cultural barriers. Call-out culture, as we first named it within Black Twitter, quickly became a strategy
to be feared, as it could not be tempered by the media forms that had
historically silenced Black dissent. Primed by the efficacy of messaging
behind #BlackLivesMatter, news media continued to follow conflict as
its news value North Star, providing an often outsized picture of the
problem of the day. As an iteration of Black Digital Resistance, calling out and canceling people on social media became a phenomenon
that very quickly cycled through the process as users identified with

the issue, participated in the discussion, affirmed each other's posts—even when we disagreed with one another—and reaffirmed the value of the online discussions by repeating them in offline lives as segments on Black radio shows and spreads in print media. Short-lived and often short-sighted moments of vindication were easily won: celebrity figures, outed in pictures that were easily retrieved from entertainment archives and the memories of people who never quite forgave their offenses, apologized for dressing up in blackface and appropriating Native dress as a costume. Bigots caught on cell phone video were fired from their jobs. Businesses like Strange Fruit PR, which showed either remarkable ignorance or malice in their branding and messaging choices, quickly changed their strategies (Callahan 2014). School principal or presidential hopeful, A-list star or Blackfamous (Harriot 2022), anyone could get it. And did.

News media has a curious preoccupation over what it means to be canceled. After angry-writing an essay in response to "The Letter on Justice and Open Debate" published by *Harper's Magazine* online in the middle of both the COVID-19 pandemic and the second wave of the Black Lives Matter movement, I thought that I'd done what I could to address how Black Digital Resistance was again forcing otherwise ignorant individuals and institutions to recognize the power dynamics that shape Black America. But the recoding of digital accountability from call-out culture to "cancel culture" was a seemingly imperceptible shift to anyone who (a) wasn't Extremely Online or (b) doesn't study the rhetorics of white dominance. Calls from producers and writers both foreign and domestic interested in covering one of the hundreds of so-called cancellations indicated that it's a secondary phenomenon worth a little more examination in this attempt at a contemporary history of Black Twitter. Rooted in Black vernacular traditions, the practices of calling folks out online quickly evolved from a practice of accountability within activist groups and later, among otherwise disempowered individuals, to the shadow of a looming moral panic around so-called cancel culture as media, social, and political elites sought to silence Black critique and protest speech. And because precious little is sacred when it comes to Black humor, there were a few laughs along the way.

CO-OPTING THE NARRATIVE

To understand the latent violence in labeling Black digital protest rhetorics as cancel culture, we must first map three critical discourses that frame our understanding of such narratives. The first is the enduring mythology of the "culture wars" articulated in the 1990s-era religious right movement and revived in the post-Obama era by far-right extremists. The second consists of the productive spaces of difference that Black feminist scholars including Audre Lorde (1997) and Patricia Hill Collins (1990) prompt us to consider in order to better identify the complexities that underpin Black women's knowledge production and dissemination, building on our critical communication practices that contribute to collective culture from individual, communal, and institutional positions within the discourse. Finally, we must consider how mainstream media news narratives reduce, envelop and produce tools for delegitimizing our struggle for inclusion in the larger fabric of American culture.

Black Americans' social and political position in the dominant public sphere has been assigned based on the logics of two primary forces: political rhetoric (from both inside and outside our own communities) and news coverage. Black people's political speech has long been a source of concern for people who enjoy prime positions of race, gender, and class within the Matrix of Domination. Our dissent is often framed as an issue of cultural difference—even to the extent of being considered culturally deviant. This formulation allows powerful actors to rely on a rote yet salient script of Black refusal to assimilate in order to frame culture as one that is to be feared, disdained, and suppressed. In this case, the script invokes the culture wars thesis of the early 1990s and gets revived with every mention of cancel culture that seeks to silence Black protest.

While contemporary public memory of culture wars rhetoric often credits politician Pat Buchanan with its articulation, the concept is best attributed to sociologist James Davison Hunter, whose book *Culture Wars: The Struggle to Define America*, published in 1991, is in itself a roadmap to understanding hegemonic perspective of "what's at stake" in public discourse:

The argument that I laid out focused primarily upon a public discourse, the public symbols and rituals surrounding that discourse and how that discourse gets polarized within competing institutions and among the elites that run them. As I argued, *public discourse is a discourse of elites.* That is where you find this conflict at its most incendiary. . . .

I find the role of elites to be extremely important, and it's precisely because of the disproportionate role that they play in framing public discussion. It's they who lead the institutions, who have the resources available to them, who have a disproportionate access to the media. It is their sound bites that frame the debate. From my vantage point, *the power of culture is the power to define reality, the power to frame the debate, and that power resides among the elites.* But they are supported in concentric circles by increasingly large numbers, though of less and less passion.

As heads of household and state, or territories often won via violent conquest and/or sex-based subjugation, wealthy white men have a vested interest in neutralizing threats to their social standing in the US's cultural, racial, and gender-based hierarchies. What Hunter, Buchanan, and others who frame liberal shifts in social norms and mores as fronts in the culture wars say is softly linked to the same parochial, racist reasoning used to keep schools segregated: this rhetoric seeks to protect American culture *as they imagine it to be,* and expresses fear that Black inclusion that veers from adherence to the preset standards will loosen their grip on social control. Thus, "cultural" struggles become a dogwhistle term wielded to imply a larger scheme of Black difference and inferiority, one that in recent history dates to the 1960s, when Black Americans demanded liberty via protest speech.

One year after the Civil Rights Act was passed, Senator Daniel Patrick Moynihan published his 1965 report "The Negro Family, The Case for National Action," a document that was initially designed to be a policy brief for President Lyndon B. Johnson as his administration advanced civil rights reforms. In it, Moynihan foretold of a coming crisis of a nation ill-equipped to support a fifth sociopolitical revolution—Black

America's ascendancy into full citizenship, with all the rights and privileges thereof. History records Moynihan, like Johnson, as a liberal politician concerned with the welfare of Black folks—to an extent. But historian James T. Patterson notes (2010) that Moynihan's writing lacked the righteous indignation that characterized Johnson's public speeches on Black equality; thus, the report was read as a damning description of the nontraditional Black family rather than an implication of white America's complicity in suppressing our freedoms.

Extant scholarship and oral history have since characterized the document as one that villainizes Black families—particularly the Black matriarchy—as a perversion of the nuclear structure espoused by white politicians on both the left and the right. But given my intellectual commitments as a Black feminist scholar, I approach the report a bit differently. In the section on "The Tangle of Pathology," where Moynihan's criticisms of Black family structure arise, I find an interesting caveat in his largely mischaracterized argument that white dominance has eliminated choice of family structure for many Black families:

> In essence, the Negro community has been forced into a matriarchal structure which, because it is to out of line with the rest of the American society, seriously retards the progress of the group as a whole, and imposes a crushing burden on the Negro male and, in consequence, on a great many Negro women as well.
>
> *There is, presumably, no special reason why a society in which males are dominant in family relationships is to be preferred to a matriarchal arrangement.* However, it is clearly a disadvantage for a minority group to be operating on one principle, while the great majority of the population, and the one with the most advantages to begin with, is operating on another. This is the present situation of the Negro. *Ours is a society which presumes male leadership in private and public affairs. The arrangements of society facilitate such leadership and reward it. A subculture, such as that of the Negro American, in which this is not the pattern, is placed at a distinct disadvantage.* (Moynihan 1965; emphasis mine)

Moynihan admits the short-sightedness of assuming patriarchy as the default condition for leadership at every level, from the interpersonal nature of the family structure to the societal and institutional levels of statecraft. But this section, which has been plucked out, paraphrased, and parroted ad-nauseam through two generations, has been narrowly interpreted through the patriarchal paradigm that this country is committed to upholding as its operating system. Thus, any other arrangement—be it the "matriarchy" decried by Robert Staples (1981), fictive kinship, or communally oriented approaches to "the Black family"—is interpreted as a threat to the very fabric of society. Moynihan's interpretation that Black family arrangements do not conform to America's social order, and thus present a problem for the larger society, has become the backdrop for contemporary efforts of ideological domination that seek to invalidate Black cultural existence, from the way our communities are structured to the dialects of our public discourse.

In the 1990s, echoing the warnings of the Moynihan report on the destruction of the Black family, political leaders on the right galvanized their voting blocs by evoking imagery of war in their calls to consolidate ranks according to intersecting interests of economic, political, and social concern. The culture wars, perhaps the country's longest-running covert civil conflict (Davis 2018), is imagined and envisioned as a struggle between those who favor white heteropatriarchal "Christian values" and those who would wrest control of the country out of the hands of its historical leadership (white men) and bend it to the whims of an increasingly liberal society that champions the rights of women, gays, and nonwhites—assumably at the expense of the ruling class. It seems every Black cultural commonplace and symbol visible to the white gaze has become a target of this rhetoric and its resultant policies. Tricia Rose chronicled how the "Black noise" of rap and hip-hop sparked a moral panic about Black music, leading to the creation of parental advisory labels (1994). Sagging pants, oversize t-shirts, and bright colors in our clothing became the subject of arbitrarily enforced dress codes. Our hairstyles were deemed "dirty" and "unprofessional," requiring legislation like the CROWN Act to defend us from discrimination in the workplace (Donahoo 2021). And foreign tongues first ridiculed our talk—African American Vernacular English—before deciding it was a linguistic delicacy and co-opting it as trendy parlance, eating up the flavor we bring to life's conversations, as bell hooks has written (1992). Yet Black political thinkers including Robin D. G. Kelley have provided significant, Black-centric analysis of Black cultural production and its misappropriation in the culture wars. Kelley has argued that so much of Blackness, right down to our "play," is a meaningful cultural form. When Black life is constrained to the point that even our familial and intragroup communications are policed by white cultural norms, we find other ways to get our point across. Including using our words to light folks up.

Perhaps what makes public accountability vis-à-vis call-out culture seem so caustic is that it comes from people who those in powerful social positions are used to ignoring. Spike Lee's lament of Simmons's choice to desecrate Tubman's life and memory was a criticism levied by a peer, someone with similar influence on the culture (Robinson 2013). And perhaps it was enough for Simmons to reconsider what he'd done. Had it remained a conversation between two Black media-makers, perhaps held in person or even via email, Simmons could have easily qualified his editorial choices, accepted Lee's criticism, and moved on. There'd have been no statement of how "hurt" he was by the outcry from Black communities. There'd have been no public realization that Black people, particularly Black women, have masterfully marshaled the resources of digital technologies as another tool in fighting racism and sexism, the uniquely insidious twin properties of misogynoir. The digital spectacle of Simmons, a multimillionaire having to contend with critics who could access his world with a few clicks through an app, demonstrated call-out culture's potential efficacy to effect change.

Within a day, Simmons pulled the video and went on an apology tour, posting his mea culpa on his own accounts, and releasing statements to the media (MTV 2013). In a statement posted to his Global Grind website, Simmons said:

In the whole history of Def Comedy Jam, I've never taken down a controversial comedian. When my buddies from the NAACP called and asked me to take down the Harriet Tubman video from the All Def Digital YouTube channel and apologize, I agreed.

I'm a very liberal person with thick skin. My first impression of the Harriet Tubman piece was that it was about what one of [the] actors said in the video, that 162 years later, there's still tremendous injustice. And with Harriet Tubman outwitting the slave master? I thought it was politically correct. Silly me. I can now understand why so many people are upset. I have taken down the video. Lastly, I would never condone violence against women in any form,[1] and for all of those I offended, I am sincerely sorry. (2013)

WHAT THREAT IS LEVIED BY PUBLIC CRITIQUE?

Calling folks out online was one of the first ways Black Twitter engaged in large-scale accountability practice. Breaking from Black cultural traditions of refusing to talk about "family business," individuals with little recourse used their accounts and followings to demand symbolic vindication through acknowledgment, absolution, and apology. Each of the hashtags and cases mentioned in this chapter is linked to a value of communal defense within Black Twitter's networks. And the commitment of communal defense is iterative, oscillating between outside threats and internal ones. While Black Twitter, writ large, uses the platform to draw attention to injustice, its networks also use it to call out harmful behavior both among other Black people and perpetuated by non-Black folks.

In 2013, Black Twitter's documented (if incidental) success with online ridicule as mediated protest cost Paula Deen her corporate sponsorships and her contract with the Food Network channel (Carter and Sung 2013), and intentionally vindicated Trayvon Martin's memory by getting Juror B37's book deal canceled. Subsequently, the process of honing Black Digital Resistance as a strategy for networked boycotting efforts was perfected through a series of cases that won varying degrees of media coverage, and, consequently, public attention.

---

1. Several Black women and women of color have raised allegations of sexual harassment and violence against Simmons. Their stories were presented in *On the Record*, a documentary produced by Kirby Dick and Amy Ziering, and aired May 2020 on HBO.

But the problem with Black Twitter's engagement in public shaming as call-out culture and its interpretation in the dominant culture's
view is embedded in its refusal to abide by that culture's rules. There are
just as many internal incidents that spark Black Twitter's engagement in
Black Digital Resistance in the network as there are outside of it. Fault
lines of gender, race, class, and generation are but a few fissures that
rupture when probed or provoked. But the foundational power dynamics that undergird these lines usually remain intact. Those with access to
capital—both monetary and social—are beneficiaries of power wielded
in ways that most in Black Twitter's numbers will never enjoy. And while
their power may not pose the same immediate threat as state violence,
influential figures, including celebrities, micro-celebrities, politicians,
and the like enjoy strange privilege in the American attention economy.
@rnb_fanatic recalled a few situations that stayed within Black Twitter's boundaries and reflected the complexity of what it means for the
network to cancel someone:

> I also like how people dismiss cancel culture as fake. Maybe we're just
> holding people accountable. Barack Obama made a comment about
> cancel culture, and I didn't like how he talked about it. I love him,
> but I was like, "wait." He was talking about how young people react to
> something, but for him, he minimized the way that people are trying
> to react to something that had happened. In his experience, he was
> an activist, a boots-on the-ground-activist, he's seeing people reacting
> on social media, he's going to have a different take on it. But it makes
> me wonder: maybe cancel culture isn't really what you think it is. And
> maybe people are saying someone's canceled and they still support
> them.
>
> There's this one guy: [@fivefifths]. People pulled up his old tweets,
> he was tweeting a lot of disparaging comments about Serena Williams.
> I think he wrote an article about it. I don't think he's recovered with
> Black Twitter, but I don't think he's hurting professionally. It's really
> interesting that he can treat a high-profile Black woman that way. I
> don't want him to think that's OK. At the same time, I don't think that
> the instance has stopped him. There's a group of people who are like,
> "I don't really mess with him anymore," but I would wonder if he feels
> that way.

Another collaborator, @kiantakey, criticized the practices as being in-flexible and limiting people's ability to grow beyond whatever choice they were being held accountable for:

> We take someone's mistake and we just blow it up in a way that doesn't allow them any grace. I'm not saying that for a Harvey Weinstein, or a Matt Lauer—they *should* be canceled. The phenomenon, one person latches onto something you've done, and another latches on to drag you down. It's one thing to hold someone accountable, it's another to make someone feel . . . I just don't agree with the premise that someone can be canceled. I still have to live my life, I still have to make money. But even then, that person has to take accountability.

Useful Anger, from Theory to Practice

Protest speech and petition are two of the five freedoms enumerated in the First Amendment, but they are curiously absent from much of the news media's criticism of so-called cancel culture. Rather than in-vestigate why individuals might call for the cancellation of a particular brand, celebrity, or institution, some move in bad faith to claim that dig-ital accountability praxis could go too far—that historical figures such as the "Founding Fathers" or acerbic comics from predigital eras could not have developed their theses and punchlines in today's civil society be-cause they'd be canceled. These colorblind interpretations of phenomena conveniently ignore the structural factors that lead otherwise disem-powered people to use their voices, amplified by digital tools, to demand accountability for a range of -isms, least of all racism and sexism. Poet Audre Lorde warned us of the false accusations that follow women's response to racism: "Everything can be used, except what is wasteful. You will need to remember this, when you are accused of destruction" (1981).

Lorde's theory of "useful anger" prompts re-examination of tech-niques such as calling out and canceling folks; that the emotional and physical reactions to racism and injustice are useful rather than wasteful, especially when channeled into action—specifically in the metaphysical work of dismantling the basic assumption that racism and the products of racism, sexism, and homophobia are immutable. Calling out and canceling translate the energy of resisting oppression into demonstrable measures to call for accountability. Where accountability is impossible, these practices demand validation. They are an extension of Black Digital Resistance with very specific root causes, even if vindication is elusive. Simmons equivocated and called out his bonafides and the influence he has (had) as a hip-hop mogul rather than simply acknowledge and accept the nature of his offense (mockery of the sexual violence and degradation inherent to chattel slavery). Thus he managed to avoid truly being held accountable for his actions. Being called out or canceled, in this regard, resulted in a few days' bad publicity, at best. While he has long positioned himself as an enlightened thinker, Simmons's statement failed to acknowledge the exact harms the skit caused, and he took no tangible reparative action. For all the fear about the damage that cancellation might have wrought, the momentary vindication won in the form of acknowledgment and superficial apology was limited at best.

Still, in the same way that white feminists aligned themselves and called on their allies to shield themselves from Black Twitter's righteous anger after being called out with hashtags like #SolidarityIsForWhite-Women and #WhiteTears, white men and media elites began to recognize that they too were susceptible to the caustic criticism levied by Black people online who refuse to abide by their rules of engagement. But outsiders with little understanding of Black vernacular traditions conflated digital practice from other spaces—such as YouTube's "drama channels," the spaces where Angele Christin and Becca Lewis (2022) note that (predominately white) influencers with large (predominately white) followings trade in Black queer rhetorics, using our slang and diction in their attempts to call one another out as they struggle for attention in a crowded entertainment field. Lacking an ability or willingness to apply critical perspective and investigate some of the root causes of Black Twitter's grievances, and our choices to use online platforms to air them with particular panache, celebrities and social media personalities often go on the offensive, denigrating Black Twitter's complaints as the work of online mobs. When Black Twitter dragged former news anchor Meghan

Kelly for proclaiming Santa Claus and Jesus were white men, she was able to use her position as a high-profile white woman—where whiteness is a cultural value signifying authority—to reduce valid and robust criticism as a performance of a certain kind of "culture," positioning it as the target of a coded racial appeal designed to silence such speech.

"The 'Black Twitter is mean to me' tears of the white feminist are a major part of the identitarian political force within mainstream white feminism," Dianna E. Anderson wrote in their 2018 book *Problematic: How Toxic Callout Culture is Destroying Feminism.*

> The idea that representatives are not following the rules of white feminism – the required levels of politeness, the conception that talking about race is racist, and those unspoken "you don't challenge this person" rules is an emulsifying force among white feminists. By lumping legitimate criticism with harassment, because it doesn't follow the rules of the dominant group, white feminism reinforces racial politics that have plagued feminism for centuries. And they force other feminists to team up with them in enforcing the perceived identity of the group label. (Anderson 2018, 81–82)

Conversely, white women's unwillingness to interrogate their own positions of power is reflected and extended in news media's tendencies to truncate the complexities woven into each instance of someone being canceled. Rather than parse through hundreds of thousands of noisy comments that may simply be tangentially related to the topic at hand, or even the work of bots chiming in using similar hashtags or phrases in effort to draw attention to a product or distraction, reporters often cherry pick the tweets that help them get additional sources on the record and present their version of events as truth to scores of readers and listeners who are otherwise removed from Black people in their everyday lives. The gloss over what it means to cancel someone online then creates a bifurcated false narrative: first, there is a loss of legitimacy in the complaints that initially arise, as well as the supporting chimes from others who have experienced similar slights. Second, and of greater harm, these reports create useful impediments to critical thinking. When public figures, politicians, and news media label every kind of online outcry as cancel culture instead of seeking the signal in the noise—*why are people upset?*—and explicitly describing what might be happening—cyberbullying, harassment, doxxing—they reduce the complexity of digital accountability practice to incoherent shouting, and often indirectly attribute it to Black people as a nameless, faceless mass. This pronouncement of deviancy, once assigned solely to Black people, is also conveniently portended to other groups. Parents upset about ongoing cases of gun violence, women protesting the leniency extended to Bill Cosby and Harvey Weinstein (among others), families of trans kids demanding their safety and protection—all become part of "the woke mob." Ultimately, any person or group that uses the techniques Black Twitter perfected in its search for accountability can easily find themselves counted on the wrong side of the us/them binary. Essentializing groups and oversimplifying their behavior is an effective tool for reinforcing the boundaries of belonging as a property of whiteness. To act in a way that could be construed as even attempting to cancel something or someone is to quickly find oneself a social pariah.

The out-group categorization of Blackness is yet again reinforced across time, technologies, and ideologies. In the digital spaces where Black feminists, and more broadly, Black people use creative rhetorics as a tool of self- and community-based defense, we are situated as outsiders by those whose race, gender, and class affords them a greater sense of privilege. In this sense, our rejection of conventional norms of debate and discussion is framed as yet another uncontrollable practice, a tendency to make us something to be feared rather than understood. But these practices far predate the norms we learn through being socialized among non-Black groups. E. Patrick Johnson deftly illustrates the personal and familial embodiment of call-out culture as a tool in crafting Black people's—and particularly Black women's—queer epistemologies. As Johnson describes, the women who raised us were our first debate coaches, teaching us the dexterity of language and imagery that allow us to fashion culturally resonant and incisive critique that's impossible to ignore.

It would be my Grandmother Mary, however, who would teach me how to "read." Like many black grandmothers, mine was full of mother wit and advice, and was known to give you a good knock upside the head when you needed it.

Grandmother's use of colorful language (e.g., "She gets on my nerves so bad it makes my ass want to cut stove wood"—who knew that asses were anthropomorphic!) was second only to her ability to size people up—in other words, to *read* people. She may have been illiterate in the literal sense of that word, but she could call a person out in a hot minute. (2011, 442)

The transference of Black vernacular traditions is so fluid and adaptive that reading has become an imprinted communication practice. It's only natural that where we go, our dialects come with us—with little regard for how they (and we) differ from the assumed norms of the space.

Initially, we referred to the practice as calling someone out, and as debates about its effectiveness roiled with Black Twitter's diverse communities, we began to refer to it (among ourselves) as call-out culture. As Brock notes, "originally a practice of Black women signifyin', [the call-out] has occasionally been mistaken for Twitter's 'mob mentality,' but it is qualitatively different: it is often a critique of systemic inequality rather than an attack against specific, individualistic transgressions" (2020, p. 220).

The Origins of Black Call-Out Culture

While #BlackLivesMatter protests—including those that demanded justice for Black people injured and killed by whites and/or police—dominated headlines about Black America between 2014 and 2016, several similarly structured discourses were circulated in an effort to reclaim Black narratives. A closer look at coverage of some of them highlights the intricacies in Black collective identity and illustrates Brock's (2020a) concepts of ratchetness and respectability as themes by which Black digital practices can be interpreted.

Take for instance #StayMayAbby and #BeckyWithTheBadGrades, two hashtags used to refute the narrative of Black intellectual inferiority. They were applied to a case debating the merits of affirmative action that was argued before the Supreme Court of the United States in June 2015 and decided in November 2016. Justice Antonin Scalia's comments during *Fisher v. University of Texas* (2013) reflect on the colorblind reasoning that a number of Black, college-educated folks have dealt with in pursuing higher education:

> There are those who contend that it does not benefit African Americans to get them into the University of Texas where they do not do well, as opposed to having them go to a less-advanced school, a slower-track school where they do well. One of the briefs pointed out that most of the black scientists in this country don't come from schools like the University of Texas . . . They come from lesser schools where they do not feel that they're being pushed ahead in classes that are too fast for them.

But rather than directly push back against Scalia during the case's arguments, it was Abigail Fisher, the white complainant, who caught Black Twitter's attention. (Fisher's case was orchestrated by Edward Blum, the businessman who bankrolled *Students for Fair Admissions, Inc., v. Harvard*, which struck down federal affirmative action in 2023). Black UT-Austin alumni posted pictures of themselves in graduation garb with a specific tell-off: #StayMadAbby (Wermund 2015; Whaley 2015). The credential-flouting quickly became a trending topic, with graduates of other schools chiming in about being underestimated by teachers, counselors, and classmates, and posting similar images. Some graduates of HBCUs—which produce 13 percent and 6 percent of all bachelor's and master's degrees (respectively) awarded to Black graduates in the United States—included Scalia's pointed comments about "lesser schools" in their posts. While Fisher had willingly participated in conservative legal schemes designed to bring an end to affirmative action, in Black Twitter's collective imagination, she became a proxy for the classmates, teachers, guidance counselors and other would-be judges of

Black intellect. The hashtags and their corresponding posts were a moment of good-natured (and well-deserved) gloating about the lawsuit's lack of merit, a comeuppance for all the smart Black kids who never had the opportunity—if we even cared to take it—to show our haters just how thoroughly they had us fucked up.

#BlackOnCampus and its predecessors, #BBUM (Being Black at Michigan), #ITooAmHarvard, and others also presented counternarratives of Black experiences in higher education (Lee 2014; Jacobs 2013). While the University of Texas' admission system remains in place, Michigan's higher education system lost its Supreme Court case in 2014, resulting in a substantial drop in the number of Black students admitted to the state's flagship university. The daily narratives of microaggressions and outright racial hostilities don't usually command the same attention from the media; they aren't as easily retrieved by sitting in on classes, hall meetings, and lunchrooms as reporters might pick up stories sitting in courtrooms. The #BlackOnCampus hashtags and all of their variations consolidated students' complaints and concerns, surfacing incidents that during the height of the Black Lives Matter movement's online prominence, users referred to as call-out culture.

Over time, some individuals reaffirmed both the utility and potential damage of this process, choosing instead to "call in" offending parties and educate them about their violation of community mores. Calling someone in, however, is a matter of true allyship across power asymmetries. Consistent with the theory that social ties have helped shape Black Twitter into a tangible phenomenon (belief that one is part of a structure and has influence within it), being an ally is akin to recognizing affective connection and relative power within any space. The privileged person must be reflexively aware of their relationship to disempowered people or groups, be willing to yield to the perspectives of that group, and they must use their power within the structures of oppression in the service of the subjugated individual or group's liberation. In one example, the actress Alyssa Milano tweeted about being called in by Brittney Packnett, a Black woman who emerged and was welcomed as a powerful activist voice during the Ferguson uprising. As more known hate groups were emboldened by racist rhetoric from the president, Milano tweeted "I don't recognize my country anymore," an admission that belied her ability to insulate herself from reality. Black Twitter was swift to respond on the timeline, pointing out how white people were seemingly just discovering racism when we'd been trying to tell them about it long before the 2016 election, before Mike Brown's body became a symbol, even before we championed the phrase #BlackLivesMatter. Milano's timeline went silent before she returned, relaying that Packnett had DM'd her to teach her in the moment:

> Seeing racism so brazenly out in the open—and news outlets giving hateful people a fucking platform; in this time—hurts my soul. BONE CRUSHING. To anyone ever hurt by racism: I'm here to learn and stand by your side and hand over the microphone and do whatever I can. And thank you, @MsPackyetti, for calling in instead of calling out. I love you for so much, but especially this. @AlyssaMilano (May 24, 2019)

When Milano thanks Packnett, she doesn't simply mention that the activist called her in—she emphasizes that Packnett did not call her *out*. Had Packnett affirmed Milano's initial admission by retweeting or quote-tweeting it on her own timeline, amplifying it for thousands of followers who otherwise might not know who the child star was, Milano would have certainly been subject to more biting critique than what was already on her timeline. More importantly, Packnett's choice to DM Milano rather than to subtweet or even tweet directly at her spared the child star a certain degree of embarrassment while upholding whatever connection the two shared. While Milano had to humble herself and be receptive to Packnett's critique in that moment, she was to do so in a comparatively intimate way, and thus avoid performing another uncomfortable reality: that people in power—especially white folks—struggle with being corrected by Black people. Among the called out and the canceled, those who push back are often responding to the idea that a someone with whom they do not share a favorable affective connection has dared to challenge their power in a public way. A common defense is to attempt to delegitimize that critique by whatever means are available—massification and anonymization are met with belittlement and scorn to dismiss "the woke mob" and its permutations rather than pausing for reflection, choosing humility, acquiescence, or well-argued refusal of the accusation. Over the years, high-powered public figures both in and outside of Black communities, including everyone from Dave Chapelle to Florida Govenor Ron DeSantis, have employed these techniques, demonstrating that among those with the ability to dominate narratives by virtue of their proximity to news media are often beyond significant public reproach.

Still, some continue to downplay the power differentials and argue that calling in is a more effective alternative. Loretta Ross, an activist credited with cocreating the term "reproductive justice," is one of the most prominent proponents of this framework, which she touted in her 2018 commencement address at Hampshire College:

> Stop spending all your time trying to persuade everybody that you know to agree with you and believe what you believe. We are not organizing cults, we are organizing a human rights movement. That's a different task.
>
> And so instead of getting people to agree with you, learn some calling-in skills so you can get people to agree to be with you, that's a different task, thinking whatever they need to think to join the human rights movement.
>
> Because all of us don't think working on women's rights is the only thing to work on, or working on queer rights is the only thing to work on, or working on the environment is the only thing to work on.
>
> I'm part of the women's rights wing of a human rights movement working with an environmental and a trans justice wing of a human rights movement. So stop acting like you're as woke as you think you are and to the extent that you think somebody else ain't woke enough, proves how unwoke you actually are.

Even Ross's definition, which she repeated in an op-ed for the *New York Times* in 2019, used rhetorical signals that were quickly consumed by Black Twitter's onlookers and reinscribed as pejoratives updated for the twenty-first century. "Woke" became to "conscious, active, and righteous" what "politically correct" was to "dignity, equity and respect"—language perverted in effort to further silence and subjugate people on the margins.

Thus an intersectional Black feminist reading of cancel culture demands that attention be paid to the articulation of dominance as the central concern. By this definition, cultural conflict is not a matter of negotiation or nuance, but one of control at the expense of the other. This is where reasoning in support of calling in perpetuates the misappropriation of call-out culture and its progeny, cancel culture. Calling in has the potential to be a liberatory practice, but it requires submission on behalf of those who are and have often historically been in dominant positions, and it is functionally antithetical to the mythology of the American way—an ethos defined by individualism and conquest.

The online discourses of racial and social justice work proved a fertile, fast-moving environment for adapting racial dog whistles of the past to an electronic frequency that would reverberate outside of Twitter and into mainstream news media coverage of the Black communities where the terminology originated. By 2020, the label had been inscribed with new meaning thanks in no small part to Black Twitter. The techniques of accountability practice honed by Black folks, particularly Black women on the platform, had since been adapted by a number of online communities to publicly critique and often castigate influential figures who might otherwise be out of reach.

CONSCRIPTED INTO THE WHITE MAN'S WAR

For Black folks, particularly Black women, the culture wars have always been about our right to live and the full expression thereof. To take up space and be seen in the way we assemble, love, worship, dress, talk, move—to exist in every way that one can *be.* Invoking "culture" as a point of separation and derision because our Black Digital Resistance discourse does not conform to white heteropatriarchal normative rules of disagreement is yet another attempt at diminishing how we articulate our concerns. Black women, and the women of Black Twitter in particular, are used to such attempts at silencing and marginalization. As I mentioned in Chapter 3 about Black women's intellectual labor on Twitter, the narrative theorizing we do to make sense of oppressive forces is not limited to our own condition. Barbara Christian refers to the banter of call-outs and cancellations as utterances of Black hieroglyphics—vivid, visible evidence of our own "race for theory . . . speculat[ing] about the nature of life through pithy language that unmask[s] the power of their world" (1987, p. 52). How else to understand the digital discourses that simultaneously identify, archive and critique expressions of power, all while imagining alternative worlds and ways of living, and usually having a good laugh at the powerful's expense?

More specifically, Christian has argued that the Other has *always* been constructed to include Black women, a point Patricia Hill Collins takes up in her explanation of how Black women's cultural production is predicated on a foundation of resistance (1989; 1990). Simply stated: Black protest, even within our own communities, has been relied upon for centuries as an ultimate expression of our agency. Whether via speech, such as Fannie Lou Hamer's testimony before the 1964 National Democratic Convention (Brooks and Houck 2011), or in action, like Florida A&M University students Wilhelmina Jakes and Carrie Patterson staging the Tallahassee bus boycott in 1956, our willingness to speak up and act out in ways that disrupt the status quo has been central to our survival (Padgett and Dawkins 1998). Indeed, protests that have erupted *within* the boundaries of Black communities, both physical and digital, which have often gone largely unnoticed by mainstream news media, are the site of critical cultural production that has helped us identify and counteract attitudes and behaviors that assume our participation in our own subjugation.

During one such internet-era occurrence in the Time Before Twitter, the women of Spelman College banded together to protest a 2004 bone-marrow drive organized by Nelly, a St. Louis rapper who aimed to find a match among students of the Historically Black women's college for his sister, who was ill with leukemia. The protestors cited the video for Nelly's "Tip Drill," which had a raunchy strip-club theme, as part of their opposition. The rapper canceled the blood drive. His sister later succumbed to the illness. The incident is one of the earliest high-profile, digital-era protests within a Black community that I can recall.

In 2014, VH1 piloted *Sorority Sisters*, a reality TV show thematically aligned with its wildly popular Black-oriented shows including *Love & Hip-Hop* and *Basketball Wives*. But the show's focus on four of the "Divine Nine"—historically Black, Greek-letter organizations—was swiftly condemned by middle-class Black viewers, including more than a few who counted themselves among Black Twitter. Shortly after the show's premiere aired, the hashtag #CancelSororitySisters was circulated on Twitter and Facebook, indexing statements from high-profile Divine Nine members (Brown 2014). Similarly, a Shea Moisture commercial equating white women's hair problems with the discrimination Black women face over their natural hair brought out Black Twitter's natural hair neighborhoods in 2017. #SheaMoistureIsCanceled trended soon after (Reed 2017). Black celebrities including Chris Brown, Kanye West, Erykah Badu, Jill Scott, and others have all been canceled for abusive or problematic actions and statements. Some, like Kevin Hart, have gone so far as to cancel themselves: after complaints about homophobic references in his tweets were pulled into Twitter conversation, the comedian resigned from hosting the 2019 Academy Awards (Daw 2020). Chrisette Michele, who performed at the 2017 presidential inauguration (Izadi 2017; Owens 2023), and actor Columbus Short (from ABC's *Scandal*), who reportedly assaulted his wife (Segarra 2022), are two notable names for whom cancellation actually stuck.

The list is endless; it is updated daily. But the invocation of the culture wars that reduce this form of accountability praxis has direct consequences for Black lives. It allows those with visibility, power, and access in the news media to collapse context around the actions and demands of those who seek accountability from people who present harm (acute, historical, or anticipated) to their community. They reduce public conversations about individual and social responsibility into "the howls of online mobs." As one of my collaborators, @RLM_3 explained:

> Things aren't credited to Black Twitter as an entity. When I heard
> about the woman who tried to get the book deal shut down

[@moreandagain], they [news media] tried to make it sound like it was one person who was disgruntled instead of a network. That's the beauty of it, there's not one leader, there's a project manager for each cause. We were *all* hurt, and she led . . . the mainstream story was not the legitimate story.

Anything that is Black sometimes feels like it has a negative connotation with it. Exposing Paula Deen's racism was under Black Twitter, but some of the things said turned people off. Is this going to be investigative journalism, social activism, or a name-and-shame? The people who don't consider themselves part of it [Black Twitter] is because they get a negative picture of it because of mainstream media coverage.

News media coverage of Black Twitter's particular penchant for canceling high-profile figures, though, does the work of reaffirming the cultural significance of its discussions, while also invoking a racial grammar that serves to delegitimize rhetorical action that fits Lorde's description of useful anger.

THE PROBLEM WITH CANCEL CULTURE

In news media's attempt to make online interactions and discourses salient to audiences outside social media, journalists have relied on the formula of creating shorthand to quickly explain complex phenomena. This often reduces competing rhetorics and the historical subjugation of marginalized voices to simple back-and-forth arguments, reproducing silence about the significance of certain cultural actions. Digital protest discourses, for instance, have earned the label of cancel culture through media framing in recent years.

Jonah Engel Bromwich, a style writer for the *New York Times*, described the digital phenomenon of being canceled as "total disinvestment in something (anything)" (2018). His story on the paper's homepage featured an embedded search engine/database that allowed users to discover whether someone or something had been canceled. As I told Bromwich, canceling is an expression of agency, a choice to withdraw one's attention from someone or something whose values, (in)action, or speech are so offensive that you no longer wish to grace them with your presence, time, or money. By 2020, the term devolved into journalistic shorthand wielded as a tool for minimizing, dismissing, and often silencing marginalized people who had adapted their earlier resistance strategies for effectiveness in the digital space.

To cancel someone online is to deprive them of one's attention, to cast aspersions on those who continue to patronize their work, and/or to symbolically blacklist them. The action is often reserved for celebrities, hinting at the relevance of a parasocial relationship between the anti-fan and the object of their attention. The celebrity may not know of the anti-fan's existence or grievance, but the anti-fan is so troubled by the celebrity's action on a particular issue that they react with what limited power they have, namely the ability to invoke protest rhetorics, social criticism, and public shaming by simply declaring the person canceled.

"Part of canceling someone is having accountability for myself," @dopegirlfresh said. Describing herself as someone who had been "extremely online" since the early aughts, she explained how the term had been extracted from its context among Black women and other people on the margins:

> It was the only way of holding someone publicly accountable and drawing a line between us and them. The second we challenge their power, they realize their shit isn't as strong as they thought.
> [For white women, the label is] short for "this is some shit Black women do to protect themselves when they have no self to protect." But canceling people isn't carcerality. When's the last time canceling hurt somebody?

The term "cancel culture" has been developed primarily by voices from the dominating sphere. The term wasn't in use among popular Black blogs such as Awesomely Luvvie, XONecole, and VerySmartBrothas before the *Times* article was published in June 2018, although the first mention of call-out culture on TheRoot.com is dated a month earlier. Anthropological labeling theory helps us to understand just how important it is to pinpoint how certain trends in non-normative behavior gain salience in the public sphere. A critique of labeling theory by Dennis Raybeck (1988) walks us through exactly what it means, from an anthropological perspective, to label an individual or group by a behavior. Howard Becker, one of the first to explicitly name labeling theory, reminds us that

> Social groups create deviance by making the rules whose infraction constitutes deviance, and by applying those rules to particular people and labeling them as "outsiders." From this point of view, deviance is not a quality of the act the person commits, but rather a consequence of the application by others of rules and sanctions to an offender. The deviant is one to whom that label has successfully been applied; deviant behavior is behavior that people so label. (1963, 9)

The process of Black Digital Resistance as accountability practice takes a text demonstrative of oppressive behavior and uses it as a clarion call to community members to seek justice. The same process of identification, self-selection, participation, affirmation, reaffirmation, and vindication that characterize Black Twitter's more humorous conversations about race, and its internal accountability practices, is revived anew. What is different is how non-Black people, and, to a larger degree, individuals at a different class rank, view these behaviors. When Christian Cooper, a Black man who was birding in New York City's Central Park, took cell phone footage of Amy Cooper (no relation) refusing to comply with the rules of the space and leash her dog, Amy Cooper called the police and claimed that Christian was harassing her (Gross 2023). This incident became an example of what so-called cancel culture looks like in action. Within hours of the video being posted to social networking platforms, including Twitter, Black users commented on it, retweeted it, and shared it with others. Black people with lived experiences like Christian Cooper's chimed in on the discussion, recalling incidents in which white people called school resources officers (police), campus security officers (also police), and neighborhood watch volunteers (wannabe police) to put them "back in their place." But what are the consequences for using the threat of law enforcement against Black people who are minding their own business? Amy Cooper's life may have been made unbearably uncomfortable for a while—because of her own actions—but the psychological harm done to men like Christian Cooper, or the children and Black people seen in countless videos being harassed by white people simply for being in the same space, doesn't fade. Worse, when white dominance insists on Black subordination at all costs, as happened when Jordan Davis was murdered by a white man for playing music too loud (Pantazi 2016; Davis and Kruger), carceral logics extend themselves in ways to further illustrate the limits of Black Digital Resistance's efficacy. Despite our most creative engagements in calling out and canceling those who harm us, nothing can restore our losses of safety and life.

#WeTriedToTellYAll: Canceling ≠ Cancel Culture

Assigning a label—particularly one that harnesses the resonance of the culture wars—is an effective tool in attempts to delegitimize the nature of Black digital protest rhetorics as a twenty-first-century evolution of our efforts to demand social change. Cancel culture is a teleological tool for silencing resistance that allows critiques of Black protest to focus on the size of the outcry, the consequences, and the pathos of "punishing" prominent figures while distracting from the conditions of power differentials, subjection, and domination that make such activity necessary. It is a misnomer for micro activism and the public performance of accountability practice. This accountability is on two levels: it is pursued from the offending party, and it is a statement of one's own values. The flattening done by news media collapses boycotting and demands for accountability into the worst of what Black existence can be in the white imaginary—collective, empowered, angry, active.

Ultimately, Black Twitter's digital rhetorics of contention illustrate the spectrum of resistance practices that have been adapted for social media platforms. Through iterative practices of Black Digital Resistance, the individuals who tweet as part of a call to action or to mobilize are engaged in the type of activism that most closely resembles the analog antecedents of protest modeled in earlier eras—whether those criticisms remain within the cultural boundaries of our own communities or extend throughout the socially constructed world.

6

Things We Lost in the (Dumpster) Fire

 **D hyphen Lee**
@DrPrimaDonna **Follow**

Just tell me where Black Twitter is going to be b/c the laughs y'all provide are therapeutic and I need that.

11:06 a.m. April 25, 2022

 73.9 K **Reply** **Copy link**

> **Read 307 replies**

The end of the workweek felt a little different for @jentrification on October 28, 2022. "I closed everything down at 6 p.m. I've said it's the longest job I've ever held. Fourteen years. I literally closed the computer down," she said. @jentrification's nearly decade-and-a-half long experience on Twitter had come to an end. On the other side of the screen, the platform's new owner had just begun his first day at the helm.

It's said that if you want to bring down a movement, you should use someone from the inside, and the Twitter saga proves this true. If anything, it wasn't cancel culture or the misrepresentation of Black

Twitter that destroyed a media ecosystem where connection to Black experiences could thrive; it was another billionaire tech founder.

As I began revising this chapter in 2022, a court had recently compelled Tesla founder Elon Musk to follow through on one of his trial-balloon tweets and actually purchase Twitter. The "will he or won't he?" chatter had grown from the day Musk tweeted his intentions in April 2022 until a federal court judge forced him to complete the deal in October of that same year. Executive leadership was forced out within a matter of days. Within two weeks, Musk had disbanded trust and safety teams, including workers responsible for content moderation and reporting policies. Some 3,700 Twitter employees—more than half of the platform's workforce—were unceremoniously laid off. Many learned about their firing when their credential for interoffice communications failed. Others, like Twitter's Africa team, based in Ghana, heard of their fate from third-party sources.

@me: OK, but what exactly makes it so bad that you've decided to leave?

@jentrification: It gives the bad actors permission. Some folks were trying to convince me to stay, but it invites all of the worst of society to pile on. We don't need to take on all of the folks who were already considered trolls, bad-faith arguments and misinformation. Other bad actors from other countries who are providing disinformation. Anyone who sees this as an opportunity to . . . The fact that this sale closed within days of a midterm election in this country.

It's what we *don't* know (about Musk's plans for the site). Jack wasn't necessarily the best person . . . but at least he provided the opportunity to give feedback. When God-Is Rivera was still with Twitter, she tapped into super users—we had Twitter Voices. We had a holiday party in December 2020—on Zoom, obviously. We saw that as an opportunity to speak—take Trump off the platform. He's spreading misinformation and getting people riled up, and Jack [Dorsey, Twitter cofounder and former CEO] was like, "no, come on guys, nothing's going to happen," and look! Not three weeks later, they're storming the Capitol.

In that instance, at least we were able to speak directly. He [Dorsey] was running a business that would allow people to lead and shape their jobs.

We don't have that with Elon. He's demonstrated he doesn't care about the employees. . .

Every action he's taken thus far indicates that he intends to be hostile. At least with Jack, we had an opportunity to speak with him about a tool he used.

Since the takeover, users have tried to guess what Twitter's degradation means for multiple publics, Black Twitter included. The flawed-but-widely accepted verification process of assigning blue check marks to accounts that were both noteworthy and able to demonstrate that the user was who they claimed to be was replaced with a for-profit model. It was a move that immediately thrust the information ecosystem into chaos, as jokesters took up residence on the platform posing as politicians and other influential figures. In a matter of days, if not hours, the ability to turn to Twitter and know that messages from accounts like state and local government agencies were verified was rendered obsolete for the low, low price of just $8 a month.

The free-speech ethos embraced by Musk and right-wing provocateurs also troubled Twitter's message flows. The 45th president of the United States, who months earlier had been booted from the platform for spreading election disinformation, was welcomed back, as were avowed white nationalists. As traditional and more well-recognized ad brands abandoned the platform, their absence was filled with "junk," as one of my collaborators observed. "It's literal junk—you can't see anything." In the last few weeks that I was able to access my primary account, I would agree. The ads on Twitter had simply become weird, and if "the algorithm" didn't know me before the takeover, we were certainly strangers now. Worst of all, I found myself locked out of my account in late 2022 after struggling with the two-factor authentication system added to the platform shortly before Musk purchased it. Like @jentrification, a number of Black Twitter folks who collaborated with me via interviews and online interactions posted send-offs and salvos, but nearly a year after the site changed ownership, a remnant remained. Now that I was on the outside looking in, I wanted to know why.

In December 2023, I held a final round of focus groups with folks who self-identified as being part of Black Twitter to get their take on what happens next. Ranging in age from nineteen to their late sixties, cis and genderfluid, straight, queer, asexual, and hailing from multiple regions of the United States, the Caribbean, and a few West African countries, each of my collaborators in these groups echoed a similar refrain: Twitter was the platform where they'd invested time and formed relationships; it was the one they'd come to trust for news and information about the world around them. Yes, the conditions were changing, but wasn't that a way of life for us? We'd do what we'd always done: hold on.

> It's like, well, I'm gonna rock with it til the wheels fall off, right? That's pretty much the energy I'm on. . . . The information divide between Twitter and other social media is massive. Like, if you look at Instagram, most of the time people are just screenshotting tweets. Or take there are videos of people discussing tweets, but that [platform] is not where we're getting our information from. If there is a hurricane or if there's a crash outside, the first thing you see is people asking, "hey, can we use this video to put it on the news?" The news? Even the news is getting its news from Twitter. So until we have a space where I can find out what the hell COVID is actually doing, where we're boycotting, and what the real-world folks like the railway workers are doing. Until I can get a space like that where I can get all that information, imma be on Twitter. (@ItsMrLittle, 2022)

Another said:

> You know, I've already put my investment of time into the Twitter platform. I'm not Gonna walk away from it as easily as I would otherwise. I'm just leaving my engagement to things that serve my interests hopefully and less the interest of parties who work against me. (@HannibalTabu)

This attitude is essential to understanding Black lived experience, and just happens to be applicable to our use of technology: we are hypervigilant about the potential for our shared social worlds to be undone because we have seen it—lived it—time and again. Precarity is inherent to Blackness being in a world defined by whiteness. This is a truth that is reinforced across realities: that we have to have "the talk," with our children, warning them about how the police may not protect us; the histories of our land being snatched away for "development" via eminent domain; the idea that racial differences—rather than racism—are to blame for health disparities that are endemic to our communities. Race is a crude heuristic for power, and when wielded by rich, powerful men like Twitter's new owner, it is applied in ways that create uncertain conditions for Black folks when social norms attempt to situate us in position at the bottom of racial hierarchies. Thus, resistance becomes a way of life. As Harvey and Moten wrote, "blackness operates as the modality of life's constant escape and takes the form, the held and errant pattern, of flight" (2013, 251).

Black Twitter's existence is a practice of fugitivity extended into the digital. It is a means of stealing away from the dominant culture's norms and expectations in full view of people and institutions defined by said culture. Not as a performance, but as our modality for life, one that is practiced in surreptitious rituals that otherwise go unnoticed or are considered unremarkable. The patterns of words and speech, of music, of thinking and creating and connection *are* Black culture, even when— especially when—others aren't watching. They are the things we say, do, and make in the privacy of our own homes and bodies when surveilled by social machinations looking to sieve off style as a commodity for the world's consumption.

As an era in Black media history, Black Twitter's place amid the platform's demise is the site of rhizomatic disruption. In this moment, Black Twitter extends the legacy of Black folks using the media tools available to us to tell our stories into three distinct directions: the challenge to create new platforms developed out of the lessons of our collective lived experience, the opportunity to develop dynamic archives of this moment, and the encouragement to advance forms of journalism and media-making that intentionally center the perspectives of a people who have routinely either been written out of history or mischaracterized in a way that distorts the historical fictions honored as journalism today.

NEW PLATFORMS

To date, none of the major social networking platforms available have the same tools and functionalities that allowed Black Twitter's networks to become visible to its own numbers and people outside of Black communities. Facebook is the virtual version of a gated community. Instagram, which once offered a fun club dynamic, is starting to look more and more like a janky strip mall replete with questionable travel agencies and sketchy weight-loss schemes. Clubhouse is a bit on-the-nose with its invitation-only infrastructure. TikTok only wishes it were Vine. YouTubers offer everything from DIY education to radical indoctrination, and one wrong click can plunge a user into a fraught tour of a digital disinformation ecosystem. From my perspective, the best of Black Twitter began to fade a few years ago when the harassment, hot-takes and hateful content became overwhelming as more and more people sought (and advertisers valued) notoriety and profitability rather than information and connection.

Twitter's many-to-many broadcast model and the uptick in Black people with smartphones created the infrastructure that fostered an "overrepresentation" of Black users on the site (translation: more Black people than anyone anticipated). Live TV gave us a common place and time to gather, reinforcing our ability to connect with one another, even as these factors inadvertently made us a spectacle online.

Yet even as Twitter was being dismantled from the inside, there were Black creatives and creators extending our legacy of making something out of nothing and improving on earlier attempts to redeem the best of Black Twitter—culture and connectivity—in the development of a new platform. One example is Spill, a visual app that "moves at the speed of the culture." The brainchild of Alphonzo Terrell and DeVaris Jackson, the app was born the night Musk took over Twitter and began firing employees. Under bright lights in the otherwise pitch-black Austin City Limits auditorium in Texas during the March 2023 AfroTech conference in Austin, Terrell spoke of the moment he and his cofounder realized they could play a role in extending the life of Black Twitter in a new era:

> It was like Thanos, your access got cut off. [I said to myself] *I have to provide for my team/my people; it's time to create.* There's nothing better than us when it comes to the culture.
>
> Our thesis is if you start by centering *us*, there is unlimited possibility.

The app debuted to an initial waitlist of more than 25,000 users. With an initial investment of $5 million, Terrell claimed it had 250,000 users as of March 2023, with another 200,000 on its waitlist. Users are taking their cues from Black Twitter's early days, organizing meetups and dubbing themselves "Spillionaires," as the company aims to use Blockchain and other decentralized financial technologies to allow creators on the platform to benefit from their own labor. This is a challenge undertaken in light of the exploitation users have suffered as a consequence of choosing to create in digital spaces. One can only hope that the lessons learned from Black Twitter will be at the center of design choices for future social networking applications. As Ruha Benjamin reminds us, "justice . . . is not a static value but an ongoing methodology that can and should be incorporated into tech design" (2019, 126).

Addressing the crowd at AfroTech, Terrell sounded as though the Spill app team has considered this perspective. When asked the Silicon Valley riddle of what problem the app was looking to solve, he answered:

> The history of not just social media, but culture—the people who create the trends are often people of color, people who come from queer communities to find each other, to find community. A lot of creators started as high school kids, come together, form these crews and you get a lot of things that come out of that. That's us. That's a reflection of our experience. We're not credited; we're often not rewarded. That's first. Second, Black women and their experience with experiencing

hate. That shouldn't be a choice you have to make: *Am I going to engage with social media or experience hate?*

Several collaborators mentioned issues of safety, harassment, and surveillance as part of their concerns about a would-be Twitter killer.

> I at least pulled down my archive a couple of weeks ago, so I've got most of what I've done off of Twitter. But somebody said, *"If you leave, then the only people left here will be spewing misinformation,"* and that was an important consideration for me, because, like I said, I've always considered myself a soldier in the data war, you know. . .
>
> I mean, my mother was a Black Panther. I'm not necessarily gonna be walking around with a shotgun like she was, you know. I worked with Black Lives Matter Los Angeles, but I'm not necessarily ready to be out on the streets getting arrested. That's not really, you know, for me, because I gotta come home and make dinner in the data war. So again, I will stay on Twitter as long as I can. If there's an audience that was is capable of hearing me and interested in hearing me, and i'll stay on Twitter as long as there's the means for me to still try to elevate the discourse as best as I can when those two possibilities are not there, or when you know it melts down technically (@HanibalTabu, 2022).

Others spoke of having to write their own scripts to deal with harassment campaigns, or taking time away from the app for long stretches in order to preserve their mental health after being overwhelmed by hateful messages or videos that loop Black death and suffering. Yet with the exception of @jentrification, none of my collaborators were willing to relinquish what power they have—the ability to remain on the platform.

Black Twitter may not be ready to give up just yet, but there's something to be said for what the Spill app—and Mastodon, and Bluesky, and Spoutible, and any number of social networking sites and apps whose developers seek to establish themselves as the rightful heir of Twitter's adoption into media culture—can't offer its users: the rich history of data that's being abandoned and rendered obsolete on the platform.

ARCHIVES

Writing about technology forces you to think about mortality—particularly how much time that particular technology has before it and all its references become obsolete. Telling a story of Black Twitter requires me to keep that in the forefront of my mind. So, too, does telling a story that was less about the platform and more about the people who chose to use it, their intentions, and their impact on the world. That began to become clear within weeks of the Ferguson uprising, when six local men involved in the protests there died within months of one another, each under questionable circumstances. With each death, pieces of the authentic narrative of what it means to resist in a city under constant surveillance and siege grew quieter.

Those who remain—like Joshua Williams, who served nearly eight years in prison for stealing a bag of chips and lighting a trash can on fire during the protests, and Brittany Ferrell, a local mother and wife whose nursing career was penalized because of her activism—are left to live out a version of the truth that is often omitted from the stories we tell about what happened in her hometown. The narratives spun out of the history we all watched in real time on our devices has softened for some. For others, like Nikki Haley, former governor of South Carolina turned presidential candidate, who claims to have lowered the Confederate flag over the state capitol after the Emmanuel Nine were slain at Bible Study, the advantage is in an ability to revise history and reposition themselves as committed to liberation, as though we on the other side of the screen have forgotten that Haley didn't act until a Black woman, Bree Newsome, and her allies organized a direct action to climb the flagpole and bring down the flag, "in the name of Jesus and (our) ancestors."

Less grimly, in the five-plus years that I've taught a course on Black Twitter, I've watched as the cultural references used to describe its existence, relationships, and pleasures have grown more obscure among the digital natives in my classroom. The passage of time and the ability to delete, erase, and edit the digital materials that link our collective memory of what Black Digital Resistance looked like over the last decade forces me to confront the question a scholar asked during one of my first professional presentations: "How will we know it was a success?"

The question is specific to the Movement for Black Lives, but as a scholar, I think of it in terms of how we will measure Black Twitter's impact on society in the years to come. Within years of its novelty being proclaimed by tech writers, a number of users and critics—no one Black, mind you—declared that Twitter was "over." The language differed from white teenagers who migrated to Facebook after deeming MySpace too "ghetto" once more Black users arrived, customizing our pages and taking up space, but the implicit message was the same: once a space becomes saturated with Black users whose online activities reflect a high degree of agency, that space loses its appeal for folks who are used to being in control of the dynamics. As social media users have known for some time, but are seeing once again, if powerful forces cannot control the narratives that spring forth through the availability of online communication, they will resort to a time-honored communication strategy that has worked to dilute and delegitimize narratives that challenge existing norms: decontextualization, erasure, and omission.

Thus the second direction that Black Twitter must take—the lesson that we must learn from previous forms of mediated Black resistance—is preservation. We must commit to doing individual and collective memory work, preserving our experiences in ways that are meaningful and significant to us.

In her devastatingly haunting book *Resurrecting the Black Body: Race and the Digital Afterlife*, Tonia Sutherland writes eloquently and precisely about the harms that may befall the digital detritus that proves the evidence of our existence after we are gone:

> When we die, we leave behind our bodies and belongings as our ancestors have for millennia, but unlike our ancestors, today we also leave behind unique footprints and a trail of digital litter scattered across our online environments. Such material—digital and digitized photos, our social media posts, our gaming worlds, our email, our text and chat exchanges—all of this detritus, from full digital records to

the most miniscule of digital traces, can be thought of as our digital remains. These digital remains are not only what we create but also what is created about and for us. (Sutherland 2023, 7)

As the digital infrastructure that allowed Black Twitter to connect with one another and come into view is being hewn apart, we are challenged to preserve our digital remains while we yet live. To engage in practices of liberatory memory work is an extension of Black Digital Resistance. It is to place shared phenomena in their proper historical and cultural and personal contexts; to make sure that the details of what transpired in and through our online connections are not blotted out or obscured; to tell that half that has not been told.

Some of this work has been undertaken by journalists and other professional media workers such as Jason Parham, whose Wired series *A People's History of Black Twitter* retold the emergence and development of the phenomenon mostly through the voices of those one would expect news media to focus on: celebrities, politicians, researchers— assumably reliable sources committed to certain codes of ethics and conduct that bind their words to the easily demonstrable and accessible, and thus true. They exist in near–real time on other platforms, like the BlackTwitterThreads account on Instagram, which curates slideshows featuring tweets and moments that struck a nerve within the meta- network, and invites users to comment and contribute to reliving our memories. There are assemblages to be made from the papers, articles (news and academic), podcasts, and documentaries that attempt to retell Black Twitter's stories in its own words. There are books like this one, and those written by Moya Bailey (2021), André Brock (2020), Sarah Florini (2019), Feminista Jones (2019), Catherine Knight Steele (2021), and so many others. But what has always been of particular interest to me, and what I hope folks who read this work will be encouraged to consider, are the small histories of people who never had thousands of followers, or perhaps were never heavy users of the platform. Their per- spectives, though, are also Black Twitter. Black Twitter archives don't have to be professionally curated and held in the Blacksonian (aka the National Museum of African American History and Culture). Personal archives of Black Twitter are as simple as the screenshots we've kept, and, if we can recall them, the stories we remember.

Perhaps what is most disappointing about the phenomenon that is (was?) Black Twitter is what's common among memories of Black media—that the memory hole is particularly unkind to our experiences. We are living in real time what it means to see your history erased. How will we make sense of the ways we learned about each other, affirmed our collective existence, organized, campaigned, laughed and simply enjoyed life when the artifacts of that existence are so easily swept away? Unlike physical archives, which might be passed down within families and community groups via photographs, program handbills, and other documents, the technology that helped bind Black Twitter together will also be—in this instance—its undoing. Nevertheless, I argue that in the same way that Black Twitter is the latest iteration of Black resistance via media, the final branch of its legacy will return us to where our inquiry began, with a recognition that like newspapers, radio shows, TV programs and other interventions before it, Black Twitter's most salient contribution to Black media history will hopefully be its influence on remaking journalism that abandons the traditions and values of white domination in media-making.

ADVANCING ADVOCACY JOURNALISM

As I've said throughout this book, Black Twitter is Black people using the platform in ways that differ from what white folks and non-Black people are used to—what scholars call "normative." But our style is what we've always had, what we've always done, no matter the medium. Samuel Russwurm and John Cornish were among the first to declare that "Black people are not a monolith" in 1827 when they published *Freedom's Journal*, the first Black newspaper printed in the States. Black radio shows offered alternatives to the whitewashed versions of reality and fiction during the Golden Era of broadcast. Magazines as thematically varied as the *Crisis, Ebony, Jet, Essence,* and *Sister 2 Sister* colored in the details missing from "mainstream" publications that erased most evidence of Black existence.

Returning to the impetus for this book, the final direction for the post-Black Twitter era is the perceptible demand for a different approach to journalism as we know it, particularly in the West. In the early years of this research, commenters often referred to Black Twitter as the twenty-first-century Black press, a label I'm compelled to reject, as the twenty-first-century Black press is alive and well via legacy media such as newspapers including the *Bay State Banner*, the *Chicago Defender*, and the *New Amsterdam News*. It is also alive and well in digital-first, Black founded and/or owned outlets such as KweliTV, the Triibe, and yes, even gossip sites such as The Shade Room. But when news workers outside of Black communities ask "What comes after Black Twitter?," the subtext is not a matter of how and where Black people will get news and information; it's the revelation of just how valuable the platform and the networks of connection it helped make visible to outsiders has been to developing stories for digital platforms. It should also be an indication of how the cultural and operational values of news media in the digital age can and should change to truly reflect a more accurate reality than the ones that are more profitable and conventional to a white imagined audience.

In our 2016 study of three communities on Twitter—Black Twitter, Asian Twitter, and Feminist Twitter—collaborators divulged what they want to see from news media: historically and culturally accurate narratives that reflect our realities. This brings me back to the five filters that Black Twitter places on news as part of its critique:

Autonomy. From the choice to refer to ourselves as a collective, and to perceive that collective as a structure worthwhile of our attention and effort, we have modeled what it means to name ourselves. Our efforts to speak for ourselves include everything from our adoption of the moniker "Black Twitter," to our engagement in the process of white-balancing and the construction of critical counterfactual, where we used the technology available to point out the truth of structural inequalities and inconsistencies that are too often left out of news media coverage in an attempt to report "objectively" rather than critically. This example should inspire news workers to examine how they are trained and socialized to simply accept everything from the word of law enforcement as truth to the erasure of history that is seemingly inconsequential when telling stories that are modified by Black identity.

Authenticity. In both texture and construction, Black Twitter has helped so many discover the richness that exists beyond the so-called public radio voice—one absent any indication of age or regional inflection, as one National Public Radio executive described it (McEaney 2019); ones that resonate as Black in both tone and form, as Ariel D. Smith (2022) writes in her work on Black podcasters. The counternarratives presented online also point users to niche sources of information informed by and curated to appeal to diverse Black audiences, which create both opportunity for new Black media producers such as Capital B and The Triibe, but also expose potential for exploitation via the repetition of misinformation that is similarly designed with cultural specificity for Black audiences. Perhaps most meaningfully, Black Twitter's conversations and community connections provide its participants to explore perspectives beyond those who have the institutional backing to position themselves as scholars. CaShawn Thompson stands as one of the clearest examples of what it means to be a scholar and a teacher drawing from lived experience and using narrative theorizing as a means of communicating that experience to others via digital technologies. When Thompson tweeted #BlackGirlsAreMagic, and engaged in years of online discussion about her intentions with the hashtag, she taught multiple publics connected to Black Twitter that our cultural heritage cannot be excised from the people and the circumstances that created it:

> Who are we without all of us? We're not going leave Keisha from down the street, we're not going to Tenisha who does hair in her kitchen. You're not going to leave us out. You're not

going to leave Ms. Barbara across the street out. I believe that
our culture originally valued every member of the community
because of who they were, not what they had. (@MsCaShawn,
2021)

In news-making, valuing members of a community for who they are
and not what they have means the same journalism educational and
occupational infrastructure that underpins the Pulitzer committee that
awarded Darnella Frazier, the teenager who recorded George Floyd's
murder as it occurred, a medal for doing journalism can and should
re-examine its criteria for admitting, supporting, and advancing the ca-
reers of Black journalists who may not fit a certain mold. Frazier's Black
witnessing made the kind of revolutionary contribution that existing
norms and expectations have suppressed among journalists who have
entered (and exited) the profession for generations. To tell our stories
accurately and fairly, we must have agency over newsmaking processes,
from reporting information to designing its presentation—and we must
be able to exercise our influence without having to conform to traditional standards that have been handed down without reflection for
decades.

Accountability. Digital accountability praxis, reduced to
so-called cancel culture, is yet another example of how Black
Twitter models accountability in media-making. Alongside
practices of showing receipts (i.e., resurfacing old tweets and
other messages that contradict a person's stated position or
beliefs), and leveraging online visibility to demand
engagement, Black Twitter has modeled accountability as
admitting knowledge of past harms or exploitation, as
@lenubienne, one of my collaborators during the December
2022 focus groups pointed out:

One of the things that I have learned from Twitter is land
acknowledgment and land back. So I thank Twitter for a
whole lot of things Black Twitter. . . because it has been
Black women on Twitter who have taught me the most over

the years, and that beautiful, you know, microcosm of us just
kind of has amplified.

Black Twitter's accountability praxis could be adapted in journalism to
ground stories in deeper histories that consider more than the conflict
of the moment, an approach that is essential to what I called reparative
journalism—news production practices that center social justice and
racial justice as a key ingredient in the construction of news. This approach goes hand in hand with Black Twitter's commitment to the value
of **Context**. As I stated in Chapter 2, news media in the United States
operates under the revisionist credo that journalism is the first draft of
history. On the contrary, as Black Twitter has proven through its critical
counterfactuals that demonstrate the impact of omitting power relations
along lines of race, gender identity, social class, sexual orientation, and
the like, Black communities and other structurally marginalized groups
have volumes of experience that news media ignores in favor of more
palatable stories.

   And finally, **Credit**. If nothing else, Black Twitter as an era of media
history demands that we recognize the contributions of Black people,
wherever we are found. The women of Black Twitter tried, for years, to
warn us about disinformation campaigns on the platform. If we were serious about credit, collaborators like Shafiqa Hudson (aka @sassycrass),
the creator of #YourSlipIsShowing, discussed in Chapter 3, who provided a strategy for identifying malicious trolls on the site, would be
employed as a technology writer or in digital security. Yet the time of
this writing, she is housing insecure, all while academics and technologists use her work, as it is cited here, as a point of reference for the hollow
claim to #ListenToBlackWomen.

IN SEARCH OF BLACK JOY

I began this research in 2012. To date, I've spent more than a decade
working on it in one way or another—as research papers and projects
in my graduate program, as my dissertation, as a series of articles and

book chapters in states ranging from abandoned drafts to well-received publications. While fixed in time in the pages of this book, the cases I explored are reflections of how digital and away-from-keyboard dynamics change with time. At least two of my first collaborators have published best-selling books in that time. @FeministaJones details her experience as a Black woman on the web, chronicling the lives of Black feminists and their use of digital and social media to make and describe new worlds in her 2019 book *Reclaiming Our Space: How Black Feminists are Changing the World from the Tweets to the Streets*. @Karnythia, half of the duo that led the online conversation #FastTailGirls, detailed in Chapters 1 and 2, wrote a detailed account of the Black feminism that is discounted by white feminists and devalued by some Black feminists and other comrades of color in *Hood Feminism: Notes from the Women that a Movement Forgot* (Kendall 2020). Some of the individuals whom I did not interview, but whose away-from-keyboard activities, chronicled on Twitter as witnesses to liberation struggles in Ferguson and other cities besieged by state power, have died. One of my collaborators is experiencing a deeply personal shift, and now identifies as nonbinary. Had I published this book on its intended schedule, their deadname would be preserved here as it is in reports of their work against organized trolls elsewhere on the web. Collectively, we have survived what feels like a lifetime of struggle chronicled on the web—and yet only a portion of that struggle and what informs our places in it are reflected in our online activity. Even less is detailed on Twitter. The racial justice protests of 2014, initially met with a mix of curiosity, hostility, and indifference, "hit different" in 2020. My colleagues who use experimental methods might say that the public was primed by the events of the Ferguson and Baltimore uprisings, among others, to be more receptive to the urgency of the methods and messages arising from the Movement for Black Lives.

The political victory that tipped the balance of the US Senate in Chapter 3 became an example of the limits of Black women's mobilization when Alabama voters elected a former college football coach to represent the state in Congress in 2020. By the 2022 midterms, he was using racist imagery of Black people to mobilize white voters to vote for right-wing candidates. That same year several women spoke

on-the-record for a documentary about the abuse they experienced at
the hands of Russell Simmons, the media mogul who was canceled over
his depiction of Harriet Tubman, detailed in Chapter 5. It was a moment
connected to another major hashtag-fueled movement, #MeToo, which
took shape online in 2016 as women adopted the hashtag Tarana Burke
created to talk about experiences of sexual violence. Pulling this book
together came in fits and starts during the Trump presidency—words
I still cannot believe describe an accurate and real part of our history,
even though I opened my eyes for 1,460 days and braced myself for the
chaos the White House occupant and his ilk wrought. The project lan-
guished for nearly two years as we somehow chose to press on as close to
usual through lockdowns triggered by the global COVID-19 pandemic
of 2020 and 2021, which have since devolved into an endemic with an
ever-mutating virus that continues to debilitate and kill.

And while I focus on constructing Black Twitter's influence on media
culture as a net positive, let's not be mistaken—it was never *all* good.
Compounding the harassment from outside Black Twitter's networks
and communities is the reality that there is plenty of harm unfolding
within our numbers, too. Black Twitter's own #MeToo unfolded in 2017
when a popular account holder, @ByeCorn, who produced offline events
such as the Bourbon Ball, was accused of sexual misconduct by women
who showed up to the parties. Long before right-wing news outlets
pursued stories of financial impropriety within the Black Lives Matter
movement, community activists in the Movement for Black Lives spoke
openly about the disconnect between those who were often quoted and
photographed and made into media representatives. As a "neighborhood," Black Girl Nerds suffered a rift in 2018 when Universal Fan Con,
an effort organized by several creatives and centered around the experiences of fans from the margins (queer, Black and of color, disabled,
etc.) had a "balloon budget" and was abruptly canceled days before it
was scheduled to begin. And in between there were dozens of cases
of harassment, intimidation, and bullying within Black Twitter—just as
there are everywhere else in the World Wide Web.

But most importantly (well, to me anyway), there was joy. Black joy,
to paraphrase Robin Costes Lewis, is Black Twitter's primary aesthetic.
And as a subgenre to Black joy, Black Twitter humor is a sublime

pleasure and sustainable resource fueling our efforts to create counternarratives to the often-problematic mainstream news and entertainment media framing of Black life, values, and culture. One of the more
challenging aspects of research within the network is capturing the
rapid-fire development of hashtags, memes, and conversations that participants create as a form of comic relief, even in the face of sobering realities both online and off. But as Lewis cautions us, "there's too much that
is actually beautiful—I mean awe-inspiring; sublime—within blackness
that we miss out on daily, if not hourly, by engaging in arguments around
the right to exist" (Lewis 2016). From #MeetMeInTemecula, a recollec-
tion of the first major Black Twitter beef, to the networked vanity (Pham
2015) of selfies posted on #BlackOutDay, to the collective compila-
tions of community highlights of #BestMomentsInBlackTwitterHistory,
to tongue-in-cheek hashtags like #DonLemonReports, #AskRachel, and
#NiggerNavy, Black Twitter's online engagement on the digital play-
ground demonstrates how humor functions as a critical value among
social media users who find provocative ways to engage in digital play.

By now, nearly more than a decade after the Manjoo article that
brought Black Twitter into mainstream media's view, we have constructed a trove of memories about the community's existence, experiences and interiority. In October 2015, Black Twitter attempted to
crowdsource a chronicle of these ephemeral events with #Greatest-
MomentsInBlackTwitterHistory, recalling the tweets, hashtags, videos,
and memes that kept us laughing over the years. Outley, Bowen,
and Pinckney (2021) link the internalized rage of Black oppression
in America to the productive energy of humor, citing as inspiration
the often-unarticulated dependent clause in a familiar passage from
James Baldwin that resurfaced during the first-wave Black Lives Matter
movement between 2014 and 2016:

> To be a Negro in this country and to be relatively conscious, is to be
> in a rage almost all the time. *So that the first problem is how to control
> that rage so that it won't destroy you.* (1961, p. 205; emphasis mine)

Like Lorde's theory of useful anger, which I applied in Chapter 3's
analysis of Black women's intellectual and emotional labor on Twitter,

anger, rage, and despair figure as three key concepts through which to understand the paradoxical nature of Black joy vis-à-vis Black Twitter. Although closely linked to the transgressive properties of Black humor, which "like other humor that arises from oppression, has provided a balm, a release of anger and aggression, a way of coping with the painful consequences of racism," as Carpio (2008) says, Black joy is independent of the forces of oppression, an epigenetic mystery that survives to this day in our choices to find community and connection with one another, and to value our creations regardless of what attention they might attract. Black joy is often regarded as part of an atomic compound—bound to our sense of loss, grief, death, and subjection. But I want to believe it exists in a molecular form; that we would and do find ways to celebrate ourselves, our lives, even absent tragedy. Brock (2020a, 2020b) describes it as *jouissance*, the French concept of ecstasy, intertwining physical pleasure and social engagement. But where I have chosen to omit a framework of libidinal economy in this book, I'm forced to seek something else as a primer for understanding Black joy in isolation. It's a difficult choice to have made—especially in light of the knowledge that nothing in the digital exists without or absent from the physical. But to reduce Black joy down to a binary—any binary—is to miss the intricacies and intimacies within our ability to care for one another. And thus I return to a question from Stuart Hall, which has guided my work on Black digital culture for years: "What is this 'Black' in Black popular culture?" The consideration of Blackness in popular culture, in media culture, and specifically, in Black Twitter, is an invitation to consider how we (Black folks as an in-group) define joy for ourselves, recognizing, but refusing to submit to external social structures and strictures that would otherwise insist we consider it only in the context of our own suffering.

WE TRIED TO TELL Y'ALL—THERE ARE BLACK PEOPLE IN THE FUTURE

Safiya Noble encourages scholars of Black digital culture to "shift discourses away from simple arguments about the liberatory possibilities of the internet toward more critical engagements with how the internet is a site of power and control over Black life," as she wrote in a 2018 essay outlining a research agenda for Intersectional Black Feminist Technology studies. The imperative is clear—critical studies of Black digital culture must recognize how the mechanisms of control developed in our physical worlds are being retrofitted to define our futures.

Yet I am confident that no matter what the technology, Black folks will find a way to use it to suit our needs and interests, and in turn, will shape its use and affordances. The alchemy we created by being on Twitter and using it in our own way can't be replicated elsewhere. This is not a truth limited to the digital sphere; it is evident throughout the history of media, from text to music to image and beyond. Our use of communicative technologies, in particular, underscores my observation about Blackchannels. The emphasis is not on the technology itself, but how we use it and our motivations for doing so. The proof is in the creativity connected to Black Twitter that has come to fruition in the years since I began working on this project. Issa Rae's writing and direction have given *The MisAdventures of Awkward Black Girl* the ultimate glow-up as over the years her talents have given birth to a book, a production company, and the HBO series *Insecure*. Through our connective capacity, Black Twitter has supported Black podcasts in ways that allow them to endure the influx of newcomers to that medium. Shows like *The Read* and *The Black Guy Who Tips* have captured new audiences and even lasted long enough to see their audiences evolve and age out. But perhaps the most fascinating outcome of Black Twitter's otherwise banal activity is how it has yielded relationships, partnerships, and community.

From @bigrelly's "Twinder," a series of retweets and call-and-response Twitter posts wherein Black followers, many of them queer, posted pictures and descriptions a la personal ads of the newspaper age, to the trend #WeMetOnTwitter, seeing Black folks connect with each other in ways that reflect our love and appreciation for one another has been one of the more rewarding parts of studying this space. The relationships are a reminder of how we will continue long after this technology becomes obsolete or otherwise played out. We'll move forward as we always have: together.

A Letter on Justice and Open Debate. (2020, July 7). *Harper's Magazine*. https://harpers.org/a-letter-on-justice-and-open-debate/.

Anderson, D. E. (2018). *Problematic: How Toxic Callout Culture Is Destroying Feminism*. Lincoln: University of Nebraska Press.

Angelou, M. (1978). *Phenomenal Woman*. New York: Random House.

Bailey, M. (2021). *Misogynoir Transformed*. New York: NYU Press.

Baldwin, J., Capouya, E., Hansberry, L., Hentoff, N., Hughes, L., & Kazin, A. (1961). "The Negro in American culture." *CrossCurrents*, 11, no. 3: 205–25.

Becker, H. (1963). *Outsiders: Studies In The Sociology of Deviance*. Glencoe, IL: The Free Press.

Benjamin, R. (2019). *Race after technology: Abolitionist tools for the new Jim code*. John Wiley & Sons.

Best, S. (2018). *None Like Us: Blackness, Belonging, Aesthetic Life*. Durham, NC: Duke University Press.

Blanchard, A. L. (2007). "Developing a Sense of Virtual Community Measure." *CyberPsychology & Behavior* 10, no. 6: 827–30.

Blanchard, A. (2011). *Sense of virtual community. In Virtual Communities: Concepts, Methodologies, Tools and Applications*, 101–15: IGI Global.

Bonilla-Silva, E. (2011). "The invisible weight of whiteness: the racial grammar of everyday life in contemporary America." *Ethnic and Racial Studies*, 35, no. 2: 173–94. https://doi.org/10.1080/01419870.2011.613997

Brand, A. N. (2022). "White masculine abjection, victimhood, and disavowal in rape culture: Reconstituting Brock Turner." *Quarterly Journal of Speech* 108, no. 2: 148–171.

Brock, A. (2012). "From the Blackhand Side: Twitter as a Cultural Conversation." *Journal of Broadcasting & Electronic Media* 56, no. 4: 529–49.

Brock, A. (2020a). 5. "Black Online Discourse, Part 2: Respectability." In Distributed Blackness, 171–209. New York: NYU Press.

Brock, A. (2020b). "Making a Way Out of No Way: Black Cyberculture and the Black Technocultural Matrix." In *Distributed Blackness*, 210–42. New York: NYU Press.

Bromwich, J. (2018, June 28). "Is It Canceled?" *New York Times*. https://www.nytimes.com/2018/06/28/style/is-it-canceled.html.

Brooks, D. E., and L. P. Hébert (2006). "Gender, Race, and Media Representation." *Handbook of Gender and Communication* 16: 297–317. https://doi.org/10.4135/9781412976053

Brooks, M. P., and D. W. Houck (eds.) (2011). *The Speeches of Fannie Lou Hamer: To Tell It Like It Is*. Jackson: University Press of Mississippi.

Brown, D. K., and S. Harlow (2019). "Protests, Media Coverage, and a Hierarchy of Social Struggle." *International Journal of Press/Politics* 24, no. 4: 508–30.

Brown, K. (2014, December 22). "VH1 Con't Cancel Sorority Sisters, Even Though Everybody Hates It." *Jezebel*. https://jezebel.com/vh1-wont-cancel-sorority-sisters-even-though-everybody-1674179912.

Callahan, Y. (2014, December 9). "Strange Fruit PR Firm is now Perennial Public Relations." *The Root*. https://www.theroot.com/strange-fruit-pr-firm-is-now-perennial-public-relations-1790885995#:~:text=The%20public%20relations%20firm%20formerly,former%20name%20of%20our%20firm.

Carpio, G. (2008). *Laughing fit to kill: Black humor in the fictions of slavery*. Oxford University Press.

Carey, T. L. (2020). "Necessary Adjustments: Black Women's Rhetorical Impatience." *Rhetoric Review* 39, no. 3: 269–86.

Carter, C. J., and C. Sung (2013, June 23). "Official: Food Network Will Not Renew Paula Deen's Contract." CNN. https://www.cnn.com/2013/06/21/showbiz/paula-deen-racial-slur/index.html.

Chappell, B. (2016, September 2). "Brock Turner Freed from Jail After Serving Half of 6-Month Sentence." NPR. https://www.npr.org/sections/thetwo-way/2016/09/02/492390163/brock-turner-freed-from-jail-after-serving-half-of-6-month-sentence.

Chatelain, M. (2020). 18. Lessons from the# FergusonSyllabus. The Academic's Handbook: Revised and Expanded, 18.

Chatman, D. (2017). "Black Twitter and the Politics of Viewing Scandal." In *Fandom: Identities and Communities in a Mediated World*, ed. J. Gray, C. Sandvoss, and C. Lee Harrington, 299–314. New York: NYU Press.

Chavers, L. (2016, January 13). "Here's My Problem with #BlackGirlMagic." *Elle*. https://www.elle.com/life-love/a33180/why-i-dont-love-blackgirlmagic/.

Christian, B. (1987). "The Race for Theory." *Cultural Critique* 6: 51–63.

Collective, C. R. (1977). The Combahee River Collective Statement.

Collins, P. H. (1989). "The Social Construction of Black Feminist Thought." *Signs* 14, no. 4: 745–73.

Collins, P. H. (1990). *Black Feminist Thought: Knowledge, Consciousness, and the Politics of Empowerment*. New York: Routledge.

Conway, J. A. (2015). *Living in a Gangsta's paradise: Dr. C. DeLores Tucker's Crusade Against Gansta Rap Music in the 1990s*. City: Scholars Press.

Cooper, B. C. (2017). *Beyond Respectability: The Intellectual Thought of Race Women*. Champaign: University of Illinois Press.

Crooks, N., King, B., Donenberg, G., & Sales, J. M. (2023). "Growing up too "fast": Black girls' sexual development." *Sex Roles*, 89, no. 3: 135–54.

Davis, M. (2018). "'Culture Is Inseparable from Race': Culture Wars from Pat Buchanan to Milo Yiannopoulos." *M/C Journal* 21, no. 5. https://doi.org/10.5204/mcj.1484.

Daw, S. (2020, January 13). "Kevin Hart's Oscar Hosting Controversy: A Complete Timeline." Billboard. https://www.billboard.com/music/awards/kevin-hart-oscar-hosting-controversy-timeline-8492982/.

Demby, G. (2020, July 24). "Scandal Creates Twitter Frenzy." NPR. https://www.stlpr.org/2013-05-20/scandal-creates-twitter-frenzy.

DeRogatis, J. (2019). *Soulless: The Case Against R. Kelly*. Abrams.

Deutsch, L. (2014, August 14). "Moment of Silence Planned with #NMOS14 to Mourn Victims, Address Police Force." Lansing State Journal. https://www.lansingstatejournal.com/story/news/world/2014/08/14/moment-of-silence-planned-with-nmos14-to-mourn-victims-address-police-force/14047917/.

DiAngelo, R. (2018). *White Fragility: Why It's So Hard for White People to Talk About Racism*. Boston: Beacon Press.

Diuguid, L. (2017, February 15). "Lewis Diuguid: Harness the Best That Our Diversity Has to Offer." Nieman Reports. https://niemanreports.org/articles/on-being-a-black-journalist/.

Dixon, T. L. (2017, December 12). "Report: A Dangerous Distortion of Our Families." Color of Change. https://colorofchange.org/wp-content/uploads/2019/05/COC-FS-Families-Representation-Report_Full_121217.pdf.

Donahoo, S. (2021). "Why We Need a National CROWN Act." *Laws* 10, no. 2: 26.

Eatman, C. (2017). "An Exploration of Black National Pan-Hellenic Council (NPHC) Sorority Membership as it Relates to Academic Achievement and Civic Engagement." PhD diss., Florida International University.

Edwards, A. A. (2019, March 15). "This Mom Went to Prison for Enrolling Her Son in a School Outside Her District." Refinery29. https://www.refinery29.com/en-us/2019/03/227024/tanya-mcdowell-college-admissions-scandal-arrested-privilege.

Eligon, J. (2014, August 25). "Michael Brown Spent Last Weeks Grappling with Problems and Promise." *New York Times*. https://www.nytimes.com/2014/08/25/us/michael-brown-spent-last-weeks-grappling-with-lifes-mysteries.html.

Fausset, R. (2020, April 28). "What We Know About the Shooting Death of Ahmaud Arbery." *New York Times*. https://www.nytimes.com/article/ahmaud-arbery-shooting-georgia.html.

Feagin, J. R. (2013). *The White Racial Frame: Centuries of Racial Framing and Counter-Framing*, 2nd ed. New York: Routledge.

Fisher v. *University of Texas*, 570 U.S. 297 (2013).

Florini, S. (2014). "Tweets, Tweeps, and Signifyin' Communication and Cultural Performance on Black Twitter." *Television & New Media* 15, no. 3: 223–37.

Florini, S. (2019). *Beyond hashtags: Racial politics and Black digital networks.* New York University Press.

Franklin, V. P., and Bettye Collier-Thomas (1996). "Biography, Race Vindication, and African-American Intellectuals: Introductory Essay." *The Journal of Negro History* 81, no. 1/4: 1–16. http://www.jstor.org/stable/2717604.

Gans, H. J. (2004). *Deciding what's news: A study of CBS evening news, NBC nightly news, Newsweek, and Time.* Northwestern University Press.

Gans, H. J. (2011). "Multiperspectival News Revisited: Journalism and Representative Democracy." *Journalism* 12, no. 1: 3–13.

Giddings, P. (2001). "Missing in Action: Ida B. Wells, the NAACP, and the Historical Record." *Meridians: Feminism, Race, Transnationalism* 1, no. 2: 1–17.

Glynn, C. (2012, April 11). "Trayvon Martin Shooting Sparks Hoodie Movement." CBS News. https://www.cbsnews.com/pictures/trayvon-martin-shooting-sparks-hoodie-movement/.

Gomer, J. (2020). *White balance: How hollywood shaped colorblind ideology and undermined civil rights.* UNC Press Books.

Gooden, S. T., and S. L. Myers (2018). "The Kerner Commission Report Fifty Years Later: Revisiting the American Dream." *RSF: The Russell Sage Foundation Journal of the Social Sciences* 4, no. 6: 1–17.

Gordon-Chipembere, N. (ed.) (2011). *Representation and Black Womanhood: The Legacy of Sarah Baartman.* New York: Palgrave Macmillan.

Griffin, R. A. (2012a). "The Disgrace of Commodification and Shameful Convenience: A Critical Race Critique of the NBA." *Journal of Black Studies* 43, no. 2: 161–85.

Griffin, R. A. (2012b). "I AM an Angry Black Woman: Black Feminist Autoethnography, Voice, and Resistance." *Women's Studies in Communication* 35, no. 2: 138–57.

Grimes, C. (2005). "Civil Rights and the Press." *Journalism Studies* 6, no. 1: 117–34.

Gross, T. (2023, June 12). "Central Park Birder Christian Cooper on Being 'a Black Man in the Natural World.'" NPR.

Gruzd, A., J. Jacobson, B. Wellman, and P. Mai (2016). "Understanding Communities in an Age of Social Media: The Good, the Bad, and the Complicated." *Information, Communication & Society* 19, no. 9: 1187–93.

Hall, S. (1993). "What is this "black" in black popular culture? Social Justice." *A Journal of Crime, Conflict and World Order*, 20, no 1: 104.

Hampshire College TV (2018, May 19). "2018 Hampshire College Commencement Ceremony (Full Ceremony) [Video]." YouTube. https://www.youtube.com/watch?v=Lz2TaaEfS8Q.

Harney, Stefano and Moten, Fred. (2013). The Undercommons: Fugitive Planning and Black Study. 1–165.

Harriot, M. (2022, February 11). "Guest Column: The Meaning of Blackfamous." *The Hollywood Reporter.* https://www.hollywoodreporter.com/news/general-news/michael-harriot-guest-column-blackfamous-1235090814/.

Harris, I. (2019, April 25). "Chikesia Clemons Survived a Brutal, Viral Arrest. Now She's Speaking Out." *Teen Vogue.* https://www.teenvogue.com/story/chikesia-clemons-recovery-following-viral-arrest.

Harris, J., & Kruger, A. C. (2022). "Be Kind But Not Too Kind": Black Males' Prosocial Behaviors in the Face of Dehumanization." *Journal of Research on Adolescence*, 32, no 2: 552–568.

Harris-Lacewell, M. (2004). *Barbershops, Bibles, and BET: Everyday Talk and Black Political Thought.* Princeton, NJ: Princeton University Press.

Harvell, K. D. (2019). "The Art of Sankofa and Re-Establishing Kujichagulia: Interrogating the Educational Past of Black Folks." In *Overcoming Challenges and Creating Opportunity for African American Male Students*, ed. J. T. Butcher, J. R. O'Connor, and F. Titus, 41–71. Hershey, PA: IGI Global.

HBO Max. (2020). *On the Record.*

Hunter, J. D. (1991). *Culture Wars: The Struggle to Define America.* New York: Avalon Publishing.

Hunter-Gault, C. (2012). *To the Mountaintop: My Journey Through the Civil Rights Movement.* New York: Macmillan.

Hutchinson, B. (2021, December 21). "Derek Chauvin Wants to Go to Federal Prison, Even Though It Means He'll Do More Time." ABC News. https://abcnews.go.com/US/derek-chauvin-federal-prison-means-hell-time/story?id=81845835.

Izadi, E. (2017, January 19). "Chrisette Michele Responds to Inauguration Performance Backlash: 'I Am Willing to Be a Bridge.'" *Washington Post.* https://www.washingtonpost.com/news/arts-and-entertainment/wp/2017/01/19/chrisette-michele-responds-to-inauguration-performance-backlash-i-am-willing-to-be-a-bridge/.

Jackson, J. M. (2019, March 13). "The Real Scandal with This College Admissions Mess Is White Privilege." *Teen Vogue.* https://www.teenvogue.com/story/education-access-black-children-parents-difficult-disadvantage.

Jackson, S. J., M. Bailey, and B. F. Welles (2020). *#HashtagActivism: Networks of Race and Gender Justice.* Cambridge, MA: MIT Press.

Jacobs, P. (2013, November 20). "Trending #BBUM Campaign Offers a Stark Look at Being A Minority Student at a Top American University." *Business Insider.* https://www.businessinsider.com/bbum-offers-a-stark-look-at-being-a-minority-student-at-a-top-american-university-2013-11.

Jenkins, H. (2006a). *Convergence Culture: Where Old and New Media Collide.* New York: NYU Press.

Jenkins, H. (2006b). *Fans, bloggers, and gamers: Exploring participatory culture.* New York: NYU Press.

Jerald, M. C., E. R. Cole, L. M. Ward, and L. R. Avery (2017). "Controlling Images: How Awareness of Group Stereotypes Affects Black Women's Well-Being." *Journal of Counseling Psychology* 64, no. 5: 487.

Johnson, E. P. (2011). "Queer Epistemologies: Theorizing the Self from a Writerly Place Called Home." *Biography* 34, no. 3: 429–46.

Jones, F. (2019). *Reclaiming Our Space: How Black Feminists are Changing the World from the Tweets to the Streets.* Boston: Beacon Press.

Karenga, M. (1995). "Making the past meaningful: Kwanzaa and the concept of sankofa. Reflections." *Narratives of Professional Helping*, 1, no. 4: 36–46.

Karenga, M. (2000). "Black Studies: A Critical Reassessment Maulana Karenga." In *Dispatches from the Ebony Tower: Intellectuals Confront the African American Experience*, ed. Manning Marable, 162–70. New York: Columbia University Press.

Kelley, R. D. (1998). *Yo'Mama's Disfunktional! Fighting the Culture Wars in Urban America.* Boston: Beacon Press.

Kendall, M. (2020). *Hood Feminism: Notes from the Women That a Movement Forgot.* London: Bloomsbury.

Knezevich, A., and K. Rector (2016, November 4). "Investigative Files Provide New Insights Into Korryn Gaines' 6-Hour Standoff with Baltimore County Police." *Baltimore Sun.* https://www.baltimoresun.com/news/investigations/bs-md-co-korryn-gaines-timeline-20161103-story.html.

Laughland, O. (2019, May 7). "Sandra Bland: Video Released Nearly Four Years After Death Shows Her View of Arrest." *The Guardian.* https://www.theguardian.com/us-news/2019/may/07/sandra-bland-video-footage-arrest-death-police-custody-latest-news.

Lee, J. (2014, March 5). "I, Too, Am Harvard Photos Tell Black Students' Stories." *USA Today.* https://www.usatoday.com/story/news/nation-now/2014/03/05/black-students-harvard-tumblr/6013023/.

Lee, L. A. (2017). "Black Twitter: A response to bias in mainstream media." *Social Sciences*, 6, no. 1: 26.

Lipscomb, A. E., Emeka, M., Bracy, I., Stevenson, V., Lira, A., Gomez, Y. B., & Riggins, J. (2019). "Black male hunting! A phenomenological study exploring the secondary impact of police induced trauma on the Black man's psyche in the United States." *Journal of Sociology*, 7, no. 1: 11–8.

Lewis, R. C. (2017). *Voyage of the Sable Venus: And Other Poems.* Knopf.

Lewis, R., and A. Christin (2022). "Platform Drama: Cancel Culture, Celebrity, and the Struggle for Accountability on YouTube." *New Media & Society* 24, no. 7: 1632–56.

Lippmann, W. (1922). "The Nature of News." In *Public Opinion*, ed. W. Lippmann, 338–57. New York: MacMillan.

Lipsitz, G. (2011). "Constituted by a Series of Contestations: Critical Race Theory as a Social Movement Commentary: Critical Race Theory: A Commemoration: Response." *Connecticut Law Review*: 122.

Lopez, G. (2015, July 18). "Sandra Bland's Mysterious Death Inspired These Tragic #IfIDieInPoliceCustody Tweets." Vox. https://www.vox.com/2015/7/18/8998185/sandra-bland-IfIDieInPoliceCustody.

Loupe, D. E. (1989). "Storming and Defending the Color Barrier at the University of Missouri School of Journalism: The Lucile Bluford Case." *Journalism History*, 16, no. 1–2: 20–31.

Lorde, A. (1997). "The Uses of Anger." *Women's Studies Quarterly* 25, no. 1/2: 278–85.

Manjoo, F. (2010, August 10). "How Black People Use Twitter." *Slate*. https://slate.com/technology/2010/08/how-black-people-use-twitter.html.

Marichal, J. (2013). "Political Facebook Groups: Micro-Activism and the Digital Front Stage." *First Monday* 18, no. 12. https://doi.org/10.5210/fm.v18i12.4653.

Marwick, A. E., and D. Boyd (2011). "I Tweet Honestly, I Tweet Passionately: Twitter Users, Context Collapse, and the Imagined Audience." *New Media & Society* 13, no. 1: 114–33. https://doi.org/10.1177/1461444810365313

McCombs, M. E., and D. L. Shaw (1972). "The Agenda-Setting Function of Mass Media." *Public Opinion Quarterly* 36, no. 2: 176–87.

McEnaney, T. (2019). *This American Voice. The Oxford Handbook of Voice Studies*, 97.

McIntosh, P. (1988). "Unpacking the Invisible Knapsack." *Gender Through the Prism of Difference* 235, no. 8.

McMillan, D. W., and D. M. Chavis (1986). "Sense of Community: A Definition and Theory." *Journal of Community Psychology* 14, no. 1: 6–23. https://doi.org/10.1002/1520-6629(198601)14:1<6::AID-JCOP2290140103>3.0.CO;2-I

Mears, B. (2014, April 23). "Michigan's Ban on Affirmative Action Upheld by Supreme Court." CNN. https://www.cnn.com/2014/04/22/justice/scotus-michigan-affirmative-action/index.html.

Montgomery, J. (2013, November). "On Marissa Alexander and the Politics of Defenseless Defense." In *2014 National Conference of Black Political Scientists (NCOBPS) Annual Meeting*.

Morgan, D. F. (2018). "Visible Black Motherhood Is a Revolution." *Biography* 41, no. 4: 856–75.

Moynihan, D. P. (1997). *The Negro Family: The Case for National Action (1965)*. Washington, DC: US Department of Labor.

MTV. (2013, August 15). "Russell Simmons Apologizes for Harriet Tubman Sex Tape Parody." MTV News. https://www.mtv.com/news/ll6jl4/russell-simmons-apologizes-for-harriet-tubman-sex-tape-parody.

Murphy, C. (2020, August 26). "Introducing Leavers: Results from a Survey of 101 Former Journalists of Color." Source. https://source.opennews.org/articles/introducing-leavers-results-survey/.

Nakamura, L. (1995). "Race In/For Cyberspace: Identity Tourism and Racial Passing on the Internet." *Works and Days* 13, no. 1–2: 181–93.

"Ohio Mom Kelley Williams-Bolar Jailed for Sending Kids to Better School District" (2011, January 25). ABC News. https://abcnews.go.com/US/ohio-mom-jailed-sending-kids-school-district/story?id=12763654#:~:text=%22When%20my%20home%20got%20broken,paying%20taxes%20to%20fund%20it.

Noble, S. U. (2016). "A future for intersectional black feminist technology studies." *Scholar & Feminist Online*, 13, no. 3: 1–8.

O'Kelly, C. G. (1982). "Black Newspapers and the Black Protest Movement: Their Historical Relationship, 1827–1945." *Phylon* 43, no. 1: 1–14.

Outley, C., Bowen, S., & Pinckney, H. (2021). "Laughing while black: Resistance, coping and the use of humor as a pandemic pastime among blacks." *Leisure Sciences*, 43, no. 1–2: 305–14.

Owens, E. (2023). *The Case for Cancel Culture: How this Democratic Tool Works to Liberate Us All*. St. Martin's Press.

Padgett, G., and M. P. Dawkins (1998). "Tallahassee's Bus Protest: The Other Boycott That Sparked the Civil Rights Movement." *Negro Educational Review* 49, no. 3: 101.

Painter, N. I. (2010). *The History of White People*. New York: Norton.

Pantazi, A. (2016, November 17). "Michael Dunn Convicted of Killing 17-Year-Old After Telling Teen to Turn Down Rap Music." *Florida Times-Union*.

Patterson, J. T. (2010). *Freedom Is Not Enough: The Moynihan Report and America's Struggle Over Black Family Life—from LBJ to Obama*. New York: Basic Books.

Penney, J., and C. Dadas (2014). "(Re) Tweeting in the Service of Protest: Digital Composition and Circulation in the Occupy Wall Street Movement." *New Media & Society* 16, no. 1: 74–90.

Perry, I. (2011, July 6). "Would Casey Anthony Be Found Guilty If She Were Black?" *TheGrio*. https://thegrio.com/2011/07/06/if-casey-anthony-was-black-would-the-verdict-be-different/.

Pham, M. H. T. (2015). "I click and post and breathe, waiting for others to see what I see." *On# FeministSelfies, outfit photos, and networked vanity. Fashion theory* 19(2), 221–241.

Rainie, H., and B. Wellman (2012). *Networked: The New Social Operating System*. Cambridge, MA: MIT Press. https://doi.org/10.7551/mitpress/8358.001.0001

Ray, R. (2022) "Forming a Racially Inclusive Sociological Imagination: Becoming a Racial Equity Learner, Racial Equity Advocate, and Racial Equity Broker." In *Systemic Racism inAmerica: Sociological Theory, Education Inequality, and Social Change*, edited by Rashawn Ray and Hoda Mahmoudi, 204–18. New York, NY: Routledge.

Raybeck, D. (1988). "Anthropology and Labeling Theory: A Constructive Critique." *Ethos* 16, no. 4: 371–97.

Reed, S. (2017, April 24). "Shea Moisture Is the Latest Company Facing Backlash for an Ad." *The Hollywood Reporter*. https://www.hollywoodreporter.com/news/general-news/shea-moisture-company-faces-backlash-ad-996902/.

Report of the National Advisory Commission on Civil Disorders (1968). Washington, DC: United States, Kerner Commission.

Rich, C. (2015). *Writing and Reporting news: A Coaching Method*. Independence, KY: Cengage Learning.

Richardson, A. V. (2020). *Bearing Witness While Black: African Americans, Smartphones, and the New Protest #Journalism*. New York: Oxford University Press.

Roberts, D. E. (1997). "Unshackling Black Motherhood." *Michigan Law Review* 95: 938.

Robinson, M. (2013, August 15). "Spike Lee Slams Russell Simmons for Producing Mock Harriet Tubman Sex Tape." *Business Insider*. https://www.businessinsider.com/spike-lee-slams-russell-simmons-for-producing-mock-harriet-tubman-sex-tape-2013-8.

Rose, T. (1994). *Black Noise: Rap Music and Black Culture in Contemporary America*. Middletown, CT: Wesleyan University Press.

Rose, T. (2013). "PUBLIC TALES WAG THE DOG: Telling Stories about Structural Racism in the Post-Civil Rights Era1." *Du Bois Review: Social Science Research on Race*, 10, no. 2: 447–69.

Ross, L. (2019, August 17). "I'm a Black Feminist. I Think Call-Out Culture Is Toxic." *New York Times*. https://www.nytimes.com/2019/08/17/opinion/sunday/cancel-culture-call-out.html.

Sanburn, J. (2014, July 22). "Behind the Video of Eric Garner's Deadly Confrontation With New York Police." *Time*. https://time.com/3016326/eric-garner-video-police-chokehold-death/.

Sarason, S. B. (1974). *The Psychological Sense of Community*. San Francisco: Jossey-Bass.

Scheidt, L. A. (2006). "Adolescent Diary Weblogs and the Unseen Audience." In *Digital Generations: Children, Young People and New Media*, ed. D. Buckingham and R. Willett, 193–210. Mahwah, NJ: Lawrence Erlbaum Associates.

Schillaci, S. (2013, August 15). "Russell Simmons Apologizes for Harriet Tubman Sex Tape Parody." *Billboard*. https://www.billboard.com/music/music-news/russell-simmons-apologizes-for-harriet-tubman-sex-tape-parody-5657590/.

Schudson, M. (1997). "Why Conversation Is Not the Soul of Democracy." *Critical Studies in Media Communication* 14, no. 4: 297–309.

Segarra, E. (2022, February 17). "Columbus Short Charged with Misdemeanors After Domestic Violence Arrest." *USA Today*. https://www.usatoday.com/story/entertainment/celebrities/2022/02/17/columbus-short-charged-misdemeanors-after-domestic-violence-arrest/6829262001/.

Shewfelt, R. (2019, May 24). "Alyssa Milano Called Out for Saying She Doesn't Recognize America Anymore: What Country Were You Living in Before Now?" Yahoo! Entertainment. https://www.yahoo.com/entertainment/alyssa-milano-called-out-for-saying-she-doesnt-recognize-her-country-anymore-what-country-were-you-living-in-before-now-191919300.html.

Shirky, C. (2008). *Here Comes Everybody: The Power of Organizing Without Organizations*. New York: Penguin.

Shoemaker, P., and S. D. Reese (1996). *Mediating the Message: Theories of Influences on Mass Media Content*, 2nd ed. New York: Longman.

Shoichet, C. E. (2014, August 13). "Missouri Teen Shot By Police Was Two Days Away from Starting College." CNN. https://www.cnn.com/2014/08/11/justice/michael-brown-missouri-teen-shot/index.html.

Siff, A., J. Millman, and J. Dienst (2014, December 4). "Grand Jury Declines to Indict NYPD Officer in Eric Garner Chokehold Death." NBC New York. https://www.nbcnewyork.com/news/local/grand-jury-decision-eric-garner-staten-island-chokehold-death-nypd/1427980/.

Smith, A. D. (2022). "The black podcaster-scholar: A critical reflection of using podcasting as methodology as a black doctoral student." *Social Media+ Society*, 8, no. 3: 20563051221117576.

Smith, J. C., and S. Phelps (eds.) (1992). *Notable Black American Women, Book II*. Independence, KY: Cengage Learning.

Staples, R. (1981). "The Myth of the Black Matriarchy." *The Black Scholar* 12, no. 6: 26–34.

"#staymadabby: How Black Graduates Responded to a Key Supreme Court Case" (2015, December 11). BBC News. https://www.bbc.com/news/blogs-trending-35065014.

Steele, C. K. (2016). "The Digital Barbershop: Blogs and Online Oral Culture within the African American Community." *Social Media+ Society* 2, no. 4: 2056305116683205.

Steele, C. K. (2018). "Black bloggers and their varied publics: The everyday politics of black discourse online." *Television & New Media*, 19, no. 2: 112–27.

Steele, C. K. (2021). "Digital black feminism." In *Digital Black Feminism*. New York University Press.

Stewart, M. (2016, May 12). "This 20-Year-Old Has the Longest Sentence from the Ferguson Protests." HuffPost. https://www.huffpost.com/entry/josh-williams-ferguson-protests-sentence_n_5732626be4b016f378978451.

Sutherland, T. (2023). *Resurrecting the Black Body: Race and the Digital Afterlife*. Berkeley: University of California Press.

Tajfel, H., Billig, M.G., Bundy, R.P. and Flament, C. (1971). "Social categorization and intergroup behaviour†." *Eur. J. Soc. Psychol.*, 1: 149–78. https://doi.org/10.1002/ejsp.2420010202.

Tajfel, H., J. C. Turner, W. G. Austin, and S. Worchel, S. (1979). "An Integrative Theory of Intergroup Conflict." *Organizational Identity: A Reader* 56, no. 65: 56–65. 9780203505984-16.

"Teen Girl Shoved to Ground by McKinney Officer at Pool Party Settles for $150K" (2018, June 24). NBC 5 Dallas-Fort Worth. https://www.nbcdfw.com/news/local/girl-pushed-by-mckinney-officer-at-pool-party-settles-for-150k/2055072/.

Torres, J., and J. González (2012). *News for All the People: The Epic Story of Race and the American Media*. London: Verso Books.

Torres, J., A. Bell, C. Watson, T. Chappell, D. Hardiman, and C. Pierce (2020). "Media 2070: An Invitation to Dream Up Media Reparations." Media 2070. https://mediareparations.org/essay/.

Turner, J., C. Sicha, K. Waldman, A. Hess, W. Paskin, J. Bouie, B. Woodruff, J. Weissmann, A. Goldman, P. Ford, and D. Kois (2014, December 17). "2014: The Year of Outrage." *Slate*. https://www.slate.com/articles/life/culturebox/2014/

12/the_year_of_outrage_2014_everything_you_were_angry_about_on_social_media.html.

Tynes, B., J. Schuschke, and S. U. Noble (2016). *The Intersectional Internet: Race, Sex, Class, and Culture Online*. Lausanne: Peter Lang.

Walker, L. A., Williams, A., Triche, J., Rainey, L., Evans, M., Calabrese, R., & Martin, N. (2022). "#StayMadAbby: Reframing affirmative action discourse and White entitlement on Black Twitter." *Journal of Diversity in Higher Education*, 15, no. 6, 716–30. https://doi.org/10.1037/dhe0000275

Wells, I. B. (1991). "A Red Record. 1895." In *Selected Works of Ida B. Wells-Barnett*, ed. Trudier Harris, 138–252. New York: Oxford University Press.

Wermund, B. (2015, December 11). "Black UT Students, Alumni Share Successes Online After Scalia Comments." *Houston Chronicle*. https://www.chron.com/local/education/campus-chronicles/article/Black-UT-students-alumni-share-successes-online-6692220.php.

Whaley, N. (2015, December 10). "#StayMadAbby Goes Off on White Woman Who Sued Against Affirmative Action Policy." BET. https://www.bet.com/article/sbbu30/staymadabby-goes-off-on-woman-against-affirmative-action.

Woodson, C. G. (1926). "Negro history week." *The Journal of Negro History*, 11(2), 239.

Young, D. G. (2023). *Wrong: How Media, Politics, and Identity Drive our Appetite for Misinformation*. Baltimore: Johns Hopkins University Press.

Zhou X., B. Wellman, and J. Yu (2011). "Egypt: The First Internet Revolt?" *Peace* 27, no. 3. http://peacemagazine.org/archive/v27n3p06.html.

INDEX

For the benefit of digital users, indexed terms that span two pages (e.g., 52–53) may, on occasion, appear on only one of those pages.

Oxford Studies in Digital Politics

Founder and Series Editor: Andrew Chadwick, Professor of Political Communication and Director of the Online Civic Culture Centre (O3C) in the Department of Communication and Media, Loughborough University